Good Times, Bad Times:

Women with Learning Difficulties Telling their Stories

Edited by Dorothy Atkinson, Michelle McCarthy,
Jan Walmsley, Mabel Cooper, Sheena Rolph, Simone Aspis,
Pam Barette, Mary Coventry and Gloria Ferris

British Library Cataloguing in Publication Data

A CIP record for this book is available from the British Library

ISBN 1 902519 18 3

© Copyright 2000 BILD Publications

BILD Publications is the publishing office of the
British Institute of Learning Disabilities
Wolverhampton Road
Kidderminster
Worcestershire
United Kingdom
DY10 3PP
Telephone: 01562 850251
Fax: 01562 851970
e-mail: bild@bild.demon.co.uk

BILD Publications are distributed worldwide by
Plymbridge Distributors Limited
Plymbridge House
Estover Road
Plymouth
United Kingdom
PL6 7PZ
Telephone: 01752 202301
Fax: 01752 202333

Acknowledgements

The editors would like to acknowledge the following:

Christine Finch, for her endlessly patient organising of editors' meetings, minutes, mailings, typing, re-typing and typing again. We could not have done it without her.

Leila Nandarkhan for her generous financial support, even though she could not be with us in person.

The Open University School of Health and Social Welfare's Research Committee, for its financial support to enable us to book and pay for meeting venues and to reimburse editors' travelling expenses.

Charmian Hayes for the illustrations.

The Department of Health for the grant which enabled us to pay for illustrations to make the book more accessible to people with learning difficulties.

John Harris at BILD for his kind encouragement and practical assistance.

Contents

Good Times, Bad Times: The Helpers' Story

A book to change the world?
by Jan Walmsley

The idea for this book began many years before its publication. Two of the people who subsequently became 'helpers', Michelle McCarthy and I, had been involved in the early 1990s in planning a conference for women involved in learning disability. We had been concerned at the absence of gender issues in policy and debates around learning difficulties. Initially the primary focus was on informing and supporting staff. However, under the influence of funders, especially the National Development Team, the conference became one for women with learning difficulties – non disabled-women were only allowed to attend if accompanied by at least two women with learning difficulties. The conference *Women First* was held in 1992 in Nottingham, England, and was inspirational. Over 200 women came, and one of the highlights, if such it can be called, was the number (40) who attended the workshop on sexual abuse, and spoke about their own experiences. However, follow-up to the event was patchy, despite many delegates expressing a wish for women's groups to be founded as a result of attending the conference (see Walmsley 1993 for a detailed account of *Women First*).

At around this time, Jan and Michelle became involved in a loose coalition of women interested in learning difficulties issues which came to be known as WILD (Women in Learning Disability). WILD was largely peopled by academics, with a small number of practitioners and an even smaller number of women with learning difficulties. Its loose construction inhibited it from developing as an effective pressure group, but an information service was set up, a network founded, and it held its own conference in London in 1994. The national remit of WILD was both a strength and a weakness. A strength, potentially, because it could become a focus for women's issues, but a weakness because meeting was almost impossible. Even academics found it difficult to obtain meeting places, time off and travelling expenses, and the difficulties of involving others were huge. However, although we did not know it at the time, as the Eastleigh WILD Group's chapter shows, the conference did have a lasting legacy in the founding of some continuing women's groups.

Frustrated at the lack of progress, Michelle and I met in 1995 and decided that producing a book might be the answer. Writing a book is a legitimate activity for academics, and it would give us cause to meet. A good book on women's issues in relation to women with learning difficulties had never been written in this way, and was much needed if WILD's cause was to be furthered. Together we brainstormed the contents and list of authors, covering a whole gamut of topics – sexuality, caring, work, politics, challenging behaviour, ethnicity and race, relationships, history. Most of the chapters were to have been written by our WILD colleagues, some (a handful) were to have input by women with learning difficulties as authors. It was a book that would draw on and contribute to research and scholarship. It was a book that would have an international dimension. It was a book that was intended to be celebratory; and it was a book which would influence practice. Looking now, as I write, at the book outline, it would probably have been a good book, and one that still needs to be written. But it was not this book.

Why did the book we planned back in 1994 change to the one that was published six years later, in the year 2000? The answer to this lies, I believe, in the influence on us of the concept of empowerment. Even as we planned the original book, it seemed wrong to be doing it without input from the 'subjects' – women with learning difficulties, mothers, front-line staff. What we were planning was an expert's book. Influenced heavily by Zarb's arguments (1992) for emancipatory rather than participatory research, we were uneasily aware that it was our project. Yes, we would involve others, but we were in the driving seat, it was our careers which potentially would be furthered by its publication – though we hoped also that we would contribute modestly to changing the world. Also, more specifically, we hoped the book would have a positive influence on changing the lives of women with learning difficulties.

It was out of this unease that the decision was made to include women with learning difficulties in the planning of the book, the editorial process, and to discover how far, within the bounds of conventional publishing and writing, we could change our modes of working to enable women with learning difficulties to do more than contribute their personal stories. How far, indeed, could we change to an emancipatory way of writing and publishing?

Changing the world from within: involving women with learning difficulties
by Dorothy Atkinson

The decision to involve women with learning difficulties in the actual writing of the book changed everything. It changed the process of writing; it transformed our meetings; and it shifted the whole style, content and design of the book itself. This has proved to be an empowering process all round, showing us all that, whatever the problems and pitfalls, women with and without learning difficulties can work together collaboratively to produce a book which speaks in many diverse voices about women's experiences.

Jan and Michelle's decision to involve women with learning difficulties in the process of writing the book was a principled one, based on their belief that women with learning difficulties should be active contributors to a project which concerned them rather than being merely the passive providers of their life stories. Their decision had the effect of opening up the book – to women with and without learning difficulties. This is where I came in: to contribute, as I first thought, to the original book proposal. But as it turned out, I contributed something quite different.

When I joined the project, other people joined too. This included Mabel Cooper, who also joined the project on the basis of the original proposal. She and I were there to co-write a chapter on the importance of life stories. We were both invited because we were already engaged in writing

Mabel's life story and this seemed a natural progression. Later on, two of Mabel's friends, Gloria Ferris and Mary Coventry, who were similarly involved in writing their own stories, also joined the group. The three of them became core members of the group. They rarely missed a meeting, and they were important in the gradual redefining of the nature and purpose of the book:

- the book was to be for *everyone*, staff and people with learning difficulties

- some of it therefore had to be *accessible* for people with learning difficulties to read for themselves, or listen to them being read out

- the book's main content was to be on personal experience, drawn from the *life stories* of women in (or attached to) the book group

- ownership of the stories belonged to their authors; women with learning difficulties were there in the capacity of helpers.

Mabel, Gloria and Mary became core members of the book group but, for long periods of time, other women with learning difficulties were members too and attended regularly; particularly the groups from Powerhouse and Opening Doors. Two individual members, Jackie Downer and Simone Aspis, came rarely but were very influential in making us stick to the principle that the book belonged to women with learning difficulties. On even rarer occasions other distant contributors, such as Susan Ashurst and Jean Andrews, came to tell or read their stories, and to listen to others being read. These occasions were both moving and memorable, and reinforced the view of many in the group that the book would – through its use of personal testimony – have the power to change the hearts and minds of key people in their lives, and in the lives of other women.

The arrival of women with learning difficulties in the group changed its focus and direction. There was no going back. The pace changed. Meetings needed to be inclusive and accessible, to involve everyone at a speed, and in a style which was respectful and empowering. This was the onerous task shared for a long time by Jan and Michelle, who chaired the meetings. They worked hard to include people in the process of discussion and planning, while also trying to keep the project moving forward. Meetings were made informal and friendly, with various attempts made to make everything as accessible as possible – illustrated notes were sometimes made and displayed on the walls as we talked; later, minutes-with-pictures were sent out to everyone to look at afterwards; and eventually we made do with brief big print size summary notes and action points to go through together in the actual meetings.

The move to accessible meetings and minutes was part of a process of sharing the project. The originators of the book, Jan and Michelle, in time relinquished their role of chairing the meetings. This task was taken on by Mabel, and marked a major shift in the ownership of the project and the book. The focus of the book had already changed to become mainly a collection of life stories, a change which was one of several brought about by the inclusion of women with learning difficulties in the group. Authorship of chapters changed, as women without learning difficulties, originally invited to be chapter authors, became instead the facilitators of chapters written/recorded by women with learning difficulties. Editing the book also became a shared endeavour, as women with learning difficulties took on the role of reading and commenting on one another's chapters, and deciding on what could and could not be included in the book.

The process of writing the book has been as important as the product. The telling and recording of stories has gone on outside the group. In my case, this has involved working in a three-way partnership with Mabel, Gloria and Mary. Mostly this has meant meeting together on the mornings of the afternoon book meetings, to work on their original stories; later, to amend them; and, later still, to add in the methods and messages. We also used these morning sessions to read and comment on other people's stories as they emerged. This meant we made a day of it, meeting in the morning and having lunch together before the book meeting started.

Our experience of working together in partnership has been mixed. On the one hand, we've had fun and become firmer friends – but on the other hand, we've had to struggle to be inclusive; to take turns to be quiet, as well as to tell stories; and to share the story-telling time out so that everyone got some. The small sub-group was complicated enough, but amicable. The large group, where decisions and negotiations had to take place, was even more complicated (and not always amicable).

The earlier meetings were sometimes torn by dissent with fundamental differences between people as to who the book was for, why we were writing it, what we wanted to say, and how best to put it over. We struggled with contradictory visions: of a scholarly book to inform people about the lives, experiences and histories of women with learning difficulties, and what these mean, versus an accessible book (or even video) of stories for other women with learning difficulties. The present book is a compromise – neither scholarly nor fully accessible, but a book rich in real-life stories for reading or listening to.

Dissent lessened when we had things to share – when there was something to show for all our efforts, all that time, all those long wrangles ... The change of mood occurred with the first of our story-reading sessions, where stories were read out and heard by a 'live' and appreciative audience. This made us into a group; a fully functioning and supportive group. Somehow, through sharing stories, everyone became a joint owner of the project and could see some point to what we were doing.

Whose voice is in the book?
by Sheena Rolph

I joined the project when it was in a stage of transition from the original idea for the book towards the form it has now taken. The project had been opened out to many more people, the meetings were large, and the debates were heated. The major issues being discussed concerned the style and type of publication, the audience, the authors, the topics, and above all the purpose of the book. It was interesting to go back to my notes taken at the first meeting I attended in July 1996, to see how ideas changed rapidly within the first year of the project.

My early notes on a proposed chapter assumed a broad-ranging historical approach, with contributions from women with learning difficulties as well as staff and others associated with their lives. It would highlight individual experiences, as well as what women have in common. It was to be written in partnership with women with learning difficulties, but I would contextualise it and analyse the major themes, drawing on my research in learning disability history. Within a few months the focus of this chapter – and of the whole book – had changed, from the helpers 'writing about and writing with women with learning difficulties' to women with learning difficulties writing most of the chapters them-selves, with support. Discussion had turned on the question: 'whose voice is in the book?' As a result a new book began to be formulated.

According to my notes, the meeting on 25 November 1996 seems to have been a turning point, when the discussion began to move the book in the direction of life stories, with many offers of contributions. It was now emphasised that the audience was to be women with learning difficulties as well as staff. In turn, this change of purpose and audience took the debate back to the original ideas, with concerns that the life stories could not stand alone, but would need to be contextualised, with commentary by supporters. Throughout, these debates were constantly steered by reminders from women with learning difficulties that 'women without learning difficulties should not take over the book' and that the book must be accessible to people with learning difficulties.

These at times cyclical arguments nearly led to an impasse, but solutions were suggested, tried, and crises averted by the gradual acceptance by all that the book was turning out to be richer and more complex than the original plan. Far from being tied into a uniform style, it would contain many styles, and many aims, and these differing contributions came to be seen as strengthening rather than weakening the book: 'Stories are told for different reasons, so this book could have different stories' (Minutes, February 1998).

Much was learned during this process of change: the women with learning difficulties volunteered skills of chairing meetings, reading and criticising one another's drafts, editing, re-drafting, having many of the key ideas, dealing with crises diplomatically; the women without learning difficulties learned lessons specifically about holding back, about inclusion and the accessibility not only of meetings and minutes but also of the book itself.

The result of the many debates was that the chapter I had originally visualised changed from being a history written mainly by me, with messages and themes drawn out by me, and contributions from Jean Andrews, my co-author, into a chapter written by Jean with my support. She also edited the chapter – as she said, 'I took bits out and put things in,' described the process of writing it, and analysed why the topic was important to her, and how her experiences might be useful to others.

We met several times to record her memories, to discuss transcripts and make changes. She – like several others involved in the project – was unable to be a regular attender at the London meetings, but she did come to a later meeting when the writing had reached an advanced stage, and she was able to participate in the reading out of her own chapter, to listen to other chapters, and, above all, to meet some of the other members of the group.

Perhaps because I had not been involved with the very beginning of the project or with the germ of the idea, I did not have to relinquish an original vision, as has been done by some of the initial core group. Seen from my later perspective – arriving as I did in the very middle of the arguments – the debates and developments, though sometimes painful, were usually positive and productive. The transition from a collaborative history to Jean's own story seemed the obvious way to go. One thing that emerged from the revised process was that when given the opportunity, many of the women with learning difficulties were able to contextualise and analyse the subjects they wrote about. When they could not, their supporter had an extended role. But it was important not to take that role for granted.

The resulting book, as it stands now, seems to offer a compromise between the collaborative work originally visualised and a complex and diverse collection of both life stories and topics which breaks new ground: the women with learning difficulties are not only the authors, they have also had editorial roles, and a major role in deciding the direction and different purposes of the book.

Joining in from a distance
by Bridget Whittell

Some of us fall into the category of more distanced 'helpers'. I am one of those people who was not able to be involved closely throughout the process, but nevertheless felt strongly committed. However, I still feel as if I have shared some of the angst, concerns and dilemmas that have been part and parcel of the book as it has evolved.

My more detached involvement mirrored that of Susan Ashurst who I helped to support in writing her contribution for the book. We shared similar reasons for not being able to come along to many meetings or play a fuller role. These included distance, lack of time, our other commitments, and lack of money to get to meetings. We both found it difficult to get to the meetings held in London together, not least because I work in North Wales during the week and Susan lives in Wigan (which is where I live as well at weekends). I think we managed it together on three occasions and on each occasion when we finally arrived back at Piccadilly Station in Manchester, we would look at one another and say: 'That was difficult!'

It was also difficult actually finding times to meet up with Susan and talk about the book, but we managed it and I know Susan feels a strong sense of achievement about having been able to tell 'her story'. A part of me has misgivings about her particular chapter, because it is a very personal and private account that is full of emotion and sadness and because I know that I would not choose to give such a personal, open account myself. It is also a very current account, with Susan telling her story as it happened. The actual telling of the story was not an easy process for either of us. Susan's need for emotional support and a listening ear was a priority, yet she also made it clear during this difficult period that this was the story she wanted to tell for the book. Times therefore needed to be sensitively negotiated during some visits, to 'tell the story for the book'. I did not always feel comfortable combining emotional support visits with 'telling the story' visits, and issues of ethics and confidentiality were a real concern. There were also dilemmas around what should and should not be included in Susan's account. I assumed responsibility for editing out certain sensitive information, but the reasons why this was done were explained to Susan and had her agreement. I did, however, feel some concern about reading and editing another woman's private and very personal story without her being able to do the same with me. However, at the same time, I respect Susan's right and choice to tell her story how she wants it told. Susan has consistently stated, all along, that she wants her side of her specific story to be told, and for people to listen to how she has been feeling during a particularly difficult time in her life.

I also feel comfortable about the way Susan 'took control' over her contribution to the book – the original ideas I had for that particular chapter went right out of the window. Susan knew exactly what she wanted to talk about, and that is what she did. Right from the very beginning it was her story, under her control. If it had been left to my control and direction, a much safer, less personal account would have been told – and I feel that would have made Susan's contribution less powerful, as well as taking away some of the author's ownership from her. I also feel some very strong messages emerge from Susan's account – and the accounts of other women included in the book – without additional context being added that is conventional with a piece of academic writing. Perhaps it was easier for me to refrain from wanting to do this because I was not there at the embryonic stages of the book where specific aims and visions were formulated.

I know from talking to Susan that being involved as a contributor to this book has given her a very real sense of achievement. The meetings we did attend together gave Susan the opportunity to meet other women involved in the book and we both enjoyed and valued that. Actually managing to make some of the meetings also helped us to feel we had a role in the book's shape and direction. I certainly felt frustrated at not being able to give more time and commitment, however, and perhaps also a sense of guilt. Yet mine was a peripheral role anyway.

I feel one of the strengths of this book is the way in which the women who had initial involvement and control, and had certain strong visions for how this book would evolve, have allowed this evolution to take a very different direction from that initially envisaged. The actual process has ended up being one of real cooperation, collaboration and compromise, although obviously tempered with difficult debates and arguments along the way. Academia generally is a very competitive environment and it is comforting and encouraging to be part of something that is more collaborative and cooperative.

It is, perhaps, worthwhile pointing out that as well as the women with learning difficulties involved in this book having different life histories and backgrounds, the same is true of the helpers. Not all of the helpers are full-time academics, and not all will regard their involvement with people with learning difficulties as being academically based. My own personal involvement with people with learning difficulties straddles both the paid and unpaid areas of my life. At a professional, paid level I am involved in full-time research concerning people with learning difficulties, which I try to conduct in as empowering a way as possible. At a personal, voluntary level, I am involved in promoting, developing and supporting advocacy, which includes providing support to a local self-advocacy group for people with learning difficulties.

This is not the first time I have co-written something with people with learning difficulties, and it will not be the last, but it is the first time I have written something just with women. The direction this book has taken has felt entirely right for me and I feel proud to have been associated with it – albeit at a distance and with less involvement, time and effort than other women have put in.

Good times, bad times: gains and losses
by Michelle McCarthy

When this writing project was first conceived by Jan Walmsley and myself in 1995, we were talking in terms of creating a rounded picture of the experiences of women involved in learning disability services. Therefore, we envisaged a book that would speak to the experiences of women with learning difficulties themselves, but also women staff, women managers or family carers. We assumed that the vast majority of contributors would be non-disabled women, although right from the start we encouraged co-writing with women with learning difficulties. We thought the book would be unique in bringing together all these perspectives in one volume and indeed it would have been. However, this vision of the book changed as has been discussed above. The book is still unique, but in a different way. It has involved the non-disabled women in the group in putting their theories of participation, inclusion and empowerment into practice. The result is a collection of stories by women with learning difficulties. The only exception to this principle is the chapter by Annemarie MacDonald, who writes about her daughter. We retained this one chapter written exclusively by the non-disabled mother of a young daughter with learning difficulties, because we thought it was important in a book about adult women to have something about the next generation, so to speak. However, Annemarie's daughter, Rose, also contributes to the book herself in words and pictures.

One of the consequences resulting from the decision to change the book in the ways described above, was that we have not (apart from Simone Aspis's introduction to Section 2 and the chapter on sexual abuse) drawn on and developed ideas from recent scholarship and research, as we had originally intended. This is because the non-disabled writers, who have access to such ideas and materials, changed their role from being authors in their own right to being the facilitators/scribes for women with learning difficulties to tell their own stories. In the chapter on sexual abuse, which I co-wrote with three women with learning difficulties, I tried to stay true to the original vision and, therefore, I made attempts to make research findings and the ideas or theories of others accessible to the women with learning difficulties.

Other consequences followed from the change of direction in the book's planning and purpose. We had originally intended the book to have an international perspective and planned to invite contributions from women in other countries. (For example, we had contacts in Canada, USA, Australia and Ireland who we thought would be interested). In the event, this did not happen, except for the chapter written by Christiane de Burg (a Belgian woman with learning difficulties). Her involvement in the book came about as a result of a chance conversation between myself and a Belgian colleague when I happened to be in Belgium for reasons unconnected with the book. The loss of an international perspective is not one which reduces the book in any way. Indeed, once the book became an anthology of individual women's life stories, it was not necessary to include women living in other countries. The richness and diversity of the accounts given by the women who are included gives the book sufficient strength to stand alone. Also the practicalities of working across different countries had to be considered: once the focus moved away from the voices of professionals to those of women with learning difficulties it became less feasible to do it. How would we make contact, and work, with 'ordinary' women with learning difficulties abroad? How would we fund the travel involved and how would we overcome the language barriers?

The original intention was that the book should have a celebratory tone, although we never wanted it to shy away from the reality of women's lives. Although the overall tone of this book is not celebratory, nevertheless the book is celebratory in other, perhaps more subtle, ways. Many of the women's accounts are about survival and overcoming prejudice and discrimination. Many of the women have managed to live meaningful and satisfying lives against the odds. In addition to the content, the process of writing this book is also something to be celebrated. It truly has been a collaborative process: women with and without learning difficulties working together in respectful and empowering ways.

Another significant change which happened along the way is that we originally spoke of the book in terms of a 'how to' book, aimed at learning disability service providers such as staff managers and planners, with the purpose of directly influencing their practice. Although we lost the 'how to' focus, nevertheless all writers were encouraged to think of key messages from their chapters, the important points they wanted people to take away and think about. These messages are quite powerful. This is, as far as I know, a unique book. Not only has it allowed women with learning difficulties to speak about their own lives, but it has done so in ways which have given them a great deal of control both over the process and the content. A similar project involving women with and without learning difficulties in Australia and Iceland and elsewhere (Johnson and Traustadottir, forthcoming) is resulting in a published book. There will no doubt be interesting similarities and differences between the two books.

The book has widened its remit since the original proposal, in that women with learning difficulties have not only been co-authors (which we always thought would be the case for at least some of the chapters) but they have also taken part in editing the volume as a whole, in chairing meetings, and in making strategic decisions about the direction of the project. While theirs have not been the only voices (it would be misleading to imply that the non-disabled women involved in this project had little or no say), their voices have been strong rather than weak and the book has gained enormously from that.

Another important change to the book from the one originally planned is the inclusion of easy-to-read chapter summaries and picture illustrations which run throughout the book. The decision to include these was an attempt to make the book as accessible as possible, both to those who actually contributed to it and to others with learning and literacy difficulties. We realise, of course, that the book can never be accessible to everyone, nor can tapes or videos. Nevertheless, we have done the best we could with the very limited resources available to us.[1]

Another important gain for the book came towards the end of the process. As well as the individual women's life stories and messages, we decided that one way to provide readers with information about the process or the project was for non-disabled women to write this introductory chapter. This was something that some of the women with learning difficulties felt strongly about. Just as we had wanted to make sure that the book allowed their voices to be heard, they wanted to make sure that our voices were also heard. The view was expressed that, 'the helpers should tell their story of the book'.

We also decided at the end that while some of the women's stories are powerful and moving and easily stand alone, we (the non-disabled women) should nevertheless attempt to provide a wider context. However, it should be noted that this represented a departure from the group's principles which was forcefully challenged by Simone Aspis. The compromise we reached was that Simone, not Jan, should write the Introduction to Section 2, 'Fighting back'. Even at the end there were productive conflicts about putting empowerment into practice. The section introductions represent an attempt to provide reflective commentary on the main themes emerging from the book. We hope, therefore, that while it is essentially an anthology of life stories and experiences of and by women with learning difficulties, the book is, through these additions, an enhanced anthology. As such, we hope it will help readers reflect on what meaning these women's stories might have for themselves and other women with or without learning difficulties.

[1] We are grateful to BILD, our publishers, for obtaining a Department of Health grant to enable us to commission illustrations.

Part I

Unfairness

Introduced by Michelle McCarthy

One of the strong themes to emerge from the accounts women with learning disabilities have given of their lives is that of the prejudice and unfairness they face. Whether in relation to their work or home lives, they have often been on the receiving end of discriminatory treatment from others. This theme runs through many of the chapters in this book, but the four chapters in this section illustrate this particularly well. Three of these relate to women's experience of paid work: 'What does equal really mean?' by Jackie Downer; 'Two pounds is not enough' by Sandra; and 'Scrub, scrub, scrub' by Jean Andrews. The fourth chapter, which reflects the theme of unfairness, is: 'Sexual abuse and women with learning disabilities' by myself, 'Anastasia', Pam and Deborah.

In 'What does equal really mean?' Jackie begins by explaining that a failure to give people credit for the things they can do leads to a loss of self-esteem and low expectations: 'When I was at school I never thought I could get a job. I thought I was good for nothing. Might get a job cleaning out toilets if I was lucky.' Her later experience of obtaining work and performing well in a job she valued shows how this improved the way she felt about herself: 'I felt good because I was doing a good job.'

Jackie is clear that she, and other people with learning disabilities, need extra time and support if they are to work on equal terms with non-disabled people. As she very succinctly puts it, 'Equal ... doesn't mean we are all the same.' She resents the fact that her special needs were not taken into account and allowances not made for the extra time she needed to feel her way into the job. She also suggests that while she was employed on the basis of her proven skills in networking and facilitating groups, these turned out not to be required in the new job. While this could happen to anybody, whether they have a learning disability or not, Jackie implies that it was particularly unfair and disappointing that an organisation specifically set up to empower people with learning disabilities seemed so unable to support one properly.

In Sandra's experience of paid work, her biggest complaint is that it is quite simply unfair and unreasonable to expect people to work a full day for just two pounds. Like many other people with learning disabilities she receives a very small amount of what are often euphemistically called 'therapeutic earnings' on top of her benefits. Most people with learning disabilities, whether they work or attend day centres, whether they live independently, in residential services or with their parents, experience poverty as an everyday lived reality (Davis et al. 1995). Sandra's strength of feeling about this comes through clearly, both in the title and the text of her story. She also illustrates once again how an organisation specifically set up to support people with special needs nevertheless manages to treat them unfairly – in her case by not providing her with any training and by reprimanding her for being late, even though she could not arrive any earlier, as her bus pass was not valid before a certain time.

In 'Scrub, scrub, scrub', Jean Andrews echoes some of Sandra's concerns with her own observations that working for little or no money is simply not fair. The work she was paid for, despite being hard physical work (not to mention being turned out of bed at the crack of dawn in order to do it!) was resented less than the work that was done for no money or other reasons, such as punishment. Jean describes how, at one point in her life, she did three jobs each day, so there is no doubt about her willing-ness and commitment to work. Unfortunately, this was not always matched by those responsible for finding her work – she describes being sent to work in an old people's home, where the conditions were horrendous. Nor was her sense of commitment shared by her supervisors, as she relates how she was picked on and reduced to tears by one factory supervisor.

The prejudices and unfairness described in the 'Sexual abuse and women with learning disabilities' chapter are of a somewhat different nature. Here, women describe being on the receiving end of verbal harassment and physical and sexual violence from men with and without learning disabilities. In addition to suffering from the same kinds of sexist treatment as other women, they also describe how their learning disability means that they face additional pressures. These include: being obliged to live with men the women had not chosen themselves and/or to whom they are not related by ties of family or affection; having to continue to share services with men with learning disabilities after they have been abused by them; seeing the perpetrator avoid any kind of punishment or sanction whatsoever; not being taken seriously by people paid to provide a support service to them or by their legal advocate; running a high risk of having their children taken into care; having their experiences invalidated through being 'invisible' to society at large. One woman describes her perception of this invisibility by addressing her comments directly to the non-disabled women who will be reading her chapter. She says, 'What do you ever see on the tele much about a disability life? Nothing! We want tele programmes about what we have in our future, not just what you have in your future.'

Easy-to-read version

Chapter 1

What does equal really mean?

by Jackie Downer with Jan Walmsley

When I was at school I never thought I could get a job. Might get a job cleaning toilets if I was lucky.

Then I got a job. I could do that job, running groups for black people with learning difficulties.

In 1996 I overstepped the mark. I got a job I couldn't handle. I was a manager in another organisation for disabled people. We were so busy doing so many different things it was unbelievable.

I had to rely on Martha (co-manager) to tell me what to do.

I never knew who was supposed to do what. At first there was no one to support me. Then there was ... but I couldn't trust her.

What does equal really mean? It doesn't mean we are all the same. At the end of the day Martha was the one in control. I left when I became ill with stress.

Now I have another job, one I can do.

Chapter 1

What does equal really mean?

by Jackie Downer with Jan Walmsley

Introduction

Jan writes: I know 'Jackie' very well. I also knew how she felt about the way she'd been treated in the job she describes here. I asked 'Jackie' if she would agree to talk about it for the book and she agreed. So we met in a cafe and she talked. I wrote down some notes of what she said, went away and wrote it all down as well as I could. 'Jackie' said she was happy with the story and later chose her own new name.

Many women with learning difficulties do work, in the home, in hospitals, in caring for others, but they are often not paid and do not get recognised for what they do.

In recent years, though, some women with learning difficulties have begun to find work in organisations which promote self-advocacy. Any organisation which is concerned with self-advocacy must take seriously the question of employing people with learning difficulties. They must practice what they preach.

This chapter is about what it is like to be a woman with learning difficulties working alongside non-disabled people in a self-advocacy organisation. I have worked in two self-advocacy organisations in three different jobs.

Jackie writes: When I was at school I never thought I could get a job. I thought I was good for nothing. Might get a job cleaning out toilets if I was lucky. Then I got a job with the Council, as a library assistant, stacking shelves. It was a six months training scheme. After that I got a job with a disability organisation. I was a part-time self-advocacy development worker. There were two of us, one woman without learning difficulties, one woman (me) with learning difficulties. I could do that job. Working with groups, running groups for black people with learning difficulties, doing outreach work and networking. I felt good because I was doing a good job.

In 1996 I overstepped the mark. I got a job I couldn't handle, with another organisation working for disabled people, especially people with learning difficulties. I was a manager there. There were two managers, me and a non-disabled woman I have called Martha.

People start with good intentions. You want it to work for everybody. But the professionals set up the job, and some professionals still hold the power. It was all meetings. I'm good at working with groups and I'm good at networking, but I didn't do those things in that job, never worked with groups. We got this work we had to finish in a certain number of months or the funding would be taken away. We were so busy doing so many different things it was unbelievable. The organisation was taking too much on, if you don't be careful you lose out, you are rushing.

When I got the job I expected to be a coordinator. It was a new job and I was the first person to do it. Deep down I don't think they had thought it through. What they wanted the person to do. I never knew who was supposed to do what.

It's a myth that people with learning difficulties can do everything any-one else can do. It takes us more time. No allowance was made for me to learn the job. At first there was no one to support me. Then there was, but I felt she wasn't there for me, she was Martha's friend. I couldn't trust her.

I would have to rely on Martha to know what to do. I had no warning. I'd go in Monday morning and she'd tell me what to do that day, that week. I like to plan my work, to know what to expect, to cover the next few days or the next few weeks. But I never knew. She'd ask me what I thought: 'What do you think about this, what do you think about that?'

No time to think. If I challenged her in a positive way, she didn't like it. If you can't say your opinion as a person with disabilities, what chance have you got, if they don't take that on board? People are silenced, they get bullied into saying nothing.

Equal opportunities, no way. I thought it was there, but it's not there. We don't value ourselves. Everyone's important in their own different ways. When you've got organisations you are always doing different things cos you want to get recognised. Focus on your team first of all, let them be appreciated. If you don't do that, where are you heading?

What does equal really mean? It doesn't mean we are all the same. If we don't recognise that, then including people with learning difficulties is doomed to failure. At the end of the day, Martha was the one in control, not people with learning difficulties. There's a danger of needing to please. If I said I was finding it hard working there she's telling me I've got to be careful what I say about it. People like me get used to it. Talk about equal opportunity, does it really exist?

I left when I became ill with stress. I was off work for several months, and finally resigned. I now have another job, one I can do, but it has its own problems. That's a story for another day.

Messages from Jackie's story
When you employ a woman with learning disabilities don't always judge us by our disability, judge us as people first and give us support in everything we do.

Be clear what you want from a person when you advertise a job.

Give people time to prepare.

Look at a person's skills and give them a chance to use those; support them in developing the skills they lack.

Make sure people have an independent support worker they can trust.

Easy-to-read version

Chapter 2
Two pounds is not enough

Sandra with Jan Walmsley

Sandra works as a receptionist. She says she is not paid enough.

Two pounds is not enough.

She can't buy anything with two pounds.

What she'd really like is

driving lessons

lots of children

But she hasn't got enough money to do these things.

Chapter 2

Two pounds is not enough

Sandra with Jan Walmsley

Introduction

Jan writes: Jackie Downer suggested that I should talk to Sandra because she has strong views on the paid work she does. I said it would be better if Jackie asked the questions because she knows Sandra well. We agreed on a set of questions and Jackie arranged for us to meet Sandra in the Pizza Hut in Brixton; Jackie asked the questions and I wrote down what Sandra said. Then I went away and wrote 'Two pounds is not enough'.

My name is Sandra. I'm 24 years old, I used to live with mum and dad. Now I live in a hostel. I'm mentally ill and I'm disabled, I'm not disabled, you know I've got learning disabilities.

I'm a receptionist at Feathers, Lambeth. It's an organisation for people with learning difficulties and mentally ill. People who go there do decorating, minor works, that's all. There's not a lot of women there, it's mostly men.

At the time I was in hospital, the Maudsley Hospital. The Hospital people found it for me. I have to do it, keep myself occupied because I haven't got nothing else to do. Can't sit at home. I like it because it gives me somewhere to go. But it's boring. I sit there and the visitors must sign the book, and I mind the telephone. No training. I just learning myself. You do get support from them, but I've just got to teach myself.

I work half past nine to five-thirty Tuesdays, Wednesdays and Fridays. I get two pounds a day. Not a lot of money. Can't do anything with two pounds. Can't finish my driving lessons, can't help my daughter. I'm planning kids next year and it's not enough. I haven't said it to them yet, but I feel like saying it: TWO POUNDS IS NOT ENOUGH. Two pounds can't really help me. What can it buy? Sanitary towels, two bars of soap. That's all. If you're like me, in my position, you need more money, to buy clothes and shoes. I'm not really paid. I'm doing labouring.

I like reception, but somewhere that's nearer for me. I go by bus and I got to change twice. I can't go on the bus before nine, because I can't use my pass before nine. So I don't get there till ten o' clock, and then they tell me off for being late for work.

I'd like another job, shop work, pricing food up, I wouldn't mind that, be more interesting. I can't be a bus driver like my sister. Easy for her, she can get any job she likes. She can type, book-keep, anything. What I need is something like that, to put food in the children's mouths, buy Pampers. I can't turn to my parents, say 'lend me fifty pounds' and I don't want to ask them. Children cost money, you see.

My mum might go to Jamaica. She's free, she ain't got us lot. I want to go to live in Jamaica. Be with my granny. It's hot. No cars like this in Jamaica, not a lot like there are here. People are friendly. The buses are packed solid. I want to bring my kids up there. I got cousins and aunties out there.

I was in the Maudsley. I am a manic depressive. All I do is dance to music and I don't eat or sleep two nights. Then I have to go into hospital, calm down. Now I take three tablets a day. Not Lithium, I wouldn't have that. Don't know what they are, though.

I met Clifford in hospital. He's 44. He can't work. He's on benefits, I kissed him in the grounds. When I go to his house now I got to do something, keep his place clean and tidy.

I want fourteen children. Don't mind if it's Clifford. All he's doing is paying the maintenance. Clifford don't want a screaming baby. We'll have our own flats and still be together. I wish I could have my own place. My mum said I'm not ready for that now. I'm going to give her a few more pounds. I want a baby of my own. But she doesn't understand what Clifford's like. When he's in his own atmosphere he's as good as gold. I like Clifford. I want to spend more time with him. Only place he's going is Jamaica. We talk about Jamaica a lot of the time.

Messages
Work's important, but we want to be paid properly for the work we do.

Remember we can only use disabled bus passes at certain times. If you forget that we might be paying more on fares than we get paid for the work.

Easy-to-read version

Chapter 3

Scrub, scrub, scrub

... bad times and good times: some of the jobs I've had in my life

Jean Andrews with Sheena Rolph

Jean Andrews wrote this chapter. She worked with a helper, Sheena Rolph. She talked into a tape-recorder and Sheena typed out what she said.

Jean, at home with the tape-recorder

Different jobs

Jean's chapter is about the different jobs she has done in her life. She worked in the hospital where she lived, bathing and feeding the children. She enjoyed this work because she likes children.

She did not enjoy the scrubbing of her ward on hands and knees in the early mornings.

She also used to work in the laundry, doing the ironing.

When she moved into the hostel, Jean did domestic work in the houses round about, and in an old people's home. She was pleased to move from these jobs to a full-time job in Macintosh's Chocolate Factory.

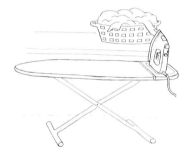

Now she works at home, running her flat with her husband. After they married they rediscovered their families who now visit them often at weekends, and Jean likes to have the flat ready for entertaining them.

Why was work important?

Jean feels that work was important to her because it helped her to leave the hospital. Once she was living in the hostel, it gave her the chance to go out to paid work.

Jean working in Macintosh's Chocolate Factory, Norwich

Jean and John at home

Why this chapter is important

Jean thinks it was important for her to write about her work. These are the reasons:

- it helps people to understand her and the sort of life she's had

- it helps people to realize that she can look after herself now.

She also thinks that reading about her life can help other people:

- it will give confidence to people who are still in hospitals and hoping to come out

- it will be useful for social workers who are helping people to leave hospitals.

Chapter 3

Scrub, scrub, scrub
... bad times and good times: some of the jobs I've had in my life

by Jean Andrews, with Sheena Rolph

Introduction
Sheena writes: I met Jean three years ago when she agreed to help me with my research into the history of learning disability. We have been meeting regularly ever since, and Jean has been telling me her life story. In the process, she has become a life historian in her own right. She suggested that we set up a group to explore the history further, and this has become an active group for change.

Jean writes: I live in a flat with my husband John. I do everything myself. I look after myself. I keep the flat clean, washing and ironing. I visit the family. I like going to the pub and meeting friends, and having friends stay the night. I just want to say that I enjoy doing research, I like it very much.

How I wrote this chapter
Sheena came here and saw me about it and we got together, didn't we. And I got to write the story, because I told the story. I told the story into the tape. Then Sheena typed it out. Then we read it together, and I took bits out and put bits in.

In the hospital: the 1950s and 1960s
I liked the work in the hospital. I used to help with the patients. I used to work on the wards when I used to be there. I used to get paid for feeding the children. I used to go back at night and feed them, with the drinks, take them round the ward. You had to feed them and make sure, wipe

their mouths because they couldn't do that. I got very friendly with Susan, one of the nurses. I've been friends with her now for years and years. I was about 19 I think when I met her. We go back a good few years. She was a good girl, really good. And I got to communicate with some of the patients, but it was a bit hard, because they couldn't speak a lot. I used to bath them and put them to bed. I loved that work, because it was the children. They needed looking after. I liked working with the children the best of all the jobs I've done, because I felt sorry for them. I enjoyed it, because I like children.

I used to start early! A nurse got us up in the morning – at six a.m.! My eyes weren't open! I needed a match stick! 'Nurse Tickle-toes' we called her. She come in the dormitory about six o' clock in the morning. Well you know what I'm like at six o' clock – one eye shut and one eye open! She used to tickle our toes and then tip us out of bed if we didn't get up. She said to me one morning, she said 'Time to get up!' 'Is it?' I say, 'I don't think so,' and I pull the sheets back over me. She pulled them off, so I pulled them back. Well she'd go round tickling your feet if you don't get up! So I wouldn't get up, I wouldn't get out of bed. So she got the mattress and tipped it on its side, on to the floor! Sergeant Major, they used to call her, because she used to go up and down, up and down. Ooh we were devils in there, we were! Mind you, we had good fun, but we used to get wrong! We had to get up early every morning to do some scrubbing on our own ward before breakfast. We all did. We had to get on our hands and knees. That was terrible. I don't know why we had to do it – I think it was just to punish us, because if you did anything wrong, you had to do it even harder! Sometimes I got het up and agitated. It's being there, I think.

We worked on other wards too, feeding, washing and dressing. We used to help the nurses. I worked with a nurse, Nurse Vail. She took me round on F6 and F3 – they were my wards. I used to make the beds. I did night duty, too. I was knackered by the time I was finished!

There was a tall lady who used to sit in this chair, and she couldn't walk, not unless you walked behind her. So I had to put my hand out to stop her from falling backwards. I had to make her walk. And I had to turn her round and put her on the toilet.

I shall never forget one poor little girl. She had a dreadful fit, and I just happened to be with her. She was all purple. And I laid her on her side, like you do a fit case, and I undone the top of her and she died. I felt ever so bad she died. I saw her die in a fit. I just didn't want it to happen.

I used to work in the laundry. I got paid for that, and I used to go to the office to collect my pay. And I used to do the sheets there, the ironing. And I used to fold up sheets and pillow cases with Mrs Jones. I got a good report from her. I didn't mind the laundry. There were two men there quite attractive! They used to chat me up in the laundry. Mind you I had to watch my step! But there wasn't anything there, why not make a life while I was in there?

Working was important because it helped us to get out (of the hospital or hostel) for good. Doing a job, helping ourselves, not doing anything wrong, it helped, I suppose. They said that if I helped and that, you know, it would probably get me out, which it did. Or I wouldn't be here, would I? I had it in my mind all the while. I knew in the end I'd get out.

The hostel
We had to work hard in the hostel, slog, slog, slog, all the while. We had to scrub the floors, lay the tables. There were no cleaners – we did the lot. We had to work hard, ever so hard. And if you do anything wrong, you got wrong, they were after you every five minutes of the day. We used to keep all the rooms clean, we used to have to do it. We used to get paid; we used to go to the office, and they used to give us a wage. But when I got a job, that was different, altogether different you know. I worked in houses, in people's houses, and Macintosh's, and places like that, you know. I used to enjoy that a bit more.

The old people's home
Before Macintosh's, I worked in an old people's home. I was there about a month. I lived in. It was in the country, right out in the blue. It was out of nowhere. I didn't know where I was, there was no-one to be seen. I don't know who got it for me. I didn't choose it, that's obvious. I mean it was not hygienic. It was horrible. Ooh! there were all these rats! They were jumping all over! The bedrooms were horrible, and there were rats everywhere. There were rats everywhere in the home.

I couldn't wash my hair, because the water was stone cold. Didn't like that job. The food was awful, you couldn't eat it! I had to clean the kitchen – great big kitchen – all hours of the night. Somebody, a woman, ran this place, and I was working all night in this blooming great old kitchen and she wouldn't let us out till we'd finished. And we had to mop all the floor, wash all the bins. I scrubbed the place, a big long corridor. Two of us went. It was terrible. You'd never believe. And them poor old people. Some of them couldn't move, some of them were terribly ill. And there were all these rats! Ooh! I shall never forget. I got hold of all these plates and I slung them on the floor and they all broke. Well, what was I supposed to do? They shouldn't have put me there in the first place.

I had a social worker and he came there and he said we had to come back to the hostel. He came up to me and he said, 'Jean, I want to speak to you,' and I said, 'What's going to happen now?' and he said, 'I've got to get you out of here, you must come out.' So I had to get out. Dr Bond had to give me a medical to make sure I was alright, because I lost a lot of weight and I started getting ill, and no wonder at it! Somebody set it up and that was really horrible. I had to come back to the hostel because I was ill. I had to have a blood test and I was anaemic. The other girl, her legs all swelled up and she had to be on hospital blocks.

I couldn't stand the job. One night the rats were all running around squeaking. I didn't know what to do. So I came back to the hostel and I had to get better. Dr Bond said I had better rest. But she said, 'You'll get out again.' But it's just one of these things. I just couldn't cope. Dr Bond was quite helpful. I sat in her office and chatted to her all about this and she said, 'You won't go back no more.' She wouldn't let me. I've been in some muddles! But I got out of them!

Domestic work
I liked my house jobs, very important. I liked those jobs.

I used to work for an elderly lady, you know. That was good, that was. She was nice, really, though a bit strict. But I got there, so there's no need to worry. I used to clean her husband's shoes! He had about six pairs of shoes a day. Mrs Phillips. I used to start at one o' clock, and finish at four. I started part-time at Macintosh's and I got this part time job in the afternoon, you see, with Mrs Phillips, and another one with Mrs Peters. What I used to do was, I used to go to Macintosh's in the morning, come home dinner time and do these other two jobs. I had my dinner at Macintosh's, then go home, and then out to work on Market Road. And you know what it's like there, very busy traffic. Crossing roads! That was the worst of it! That traffic got on my nerves. I used to dread crossing the road. When it came to crossing roads, I had to get myself out of it, because that was making me nervous even more to think I'd got to be out in the world on my own. Yes. It was the worst thing in my life. Cars. I just couldn't figure it. Getting across the road, and these cars were coming, coming up to you. Because I'd had no traffic where I was, did I? They didn't have any crossings over Market Road. How on earth did I get over that road? I helped myself. I had to do it myself. Oh it was terrible. And I thought, 'Oh my goodness, I'll never do it!'

Mrs Phillips was always there when I arrived. For her I used to do cleaning up, cleaning the house, dusting, and things like that. Mr Phillips used to walk his dirty feet all over the kitchen floor after I'd cleaned it! Mud! Especially in winter. I used to have to do it again: 'There must be no marks left on the floor!' Sometimes she said I hadn't cleaned properly. I liked it because she'd give you a break at three o' clock and we used to sit down and talk and have a cup of tea. I liked that. Sometimes she used to pop out and leave me in the house on my own.

And there used to be another lady as well, Mrs Peters. She was nice. She was an elderly lady who lived on her own and she had a cat, a black and white one. I used to go to those two on Tuesdays and Wednesdays. So I was working nearly every day and all day, really, till I went full-time at Macintosh's, and then I had to pack these two jobs up. I couldn't do them as well.

I went full-time to Macintosh's, because I couldn't see any sense in doing only two days full-time and the rest of them part-time. That's why I went, because I got a bit more money. I wanted to do that. The two ladies couldn't pay me so much. I was doing three jobs at once before, really. I cut myself in half! I didn't know where I was! But I got through it. I had to rush here, rush there, get a bus from the hostel up to Market Road, and then I had to cross that road. Ooh! all that traffic!

Macintosh's
I got a bus to Macintosh's at seven o' clock in the morning. I used to be in at half past seven and I used to go to the canteen and have a coffee up there. I used to be early clocking in with my clocking-in card. Several of us went from the hostel, so it wasn't so bad. I had to be up before six o' clock, by the time I'd washed and got ready and had my breakfast and got my things all ready.

I hated it at Macintosh' s, really hated it you know. There was a charge hand there, Cissy, and she got on to me, and then I couldn't stick any more of it. I held my temper or I'd have got the sack. She was the reason I got out. I'm not having anyone treading on me, oh no! She said I didn't clean properly. She used to make me howl. I used to go into the Tank Room and cry.

There was chocolate everywhere. I got it all over my clothes! I used to sit beside the Rolo conveyor belt, pushing them along.

I met my friend Ann there. She used to be in the Box Room. She and her husband come to see me very often now. They're quite good friends, because I made good friends with them at Macintosh's, and we kept in contact. I used to do the cleaning in the Wrapping Room. There was an Enrobing Room, and a Box Room, and a Rolo Room, and there was a Caramac Room right through the other end. And then there was the Egg Belt – great long thing – for the chocolate eggs. You just put the Rolos in the boxes. They taught me to do that, stand on the machine and do it. You had a table where you put the box on, and the sellotape on. I didn't mind that. I was only on it for a little while, though, to relieve somebody. Then I went to the Egg Belt – right to the top.

I cleaned all these places. Oh! You had to go up and down steps, up and down cleaning the chocolate off the floor, all cleaning up, sorting out all the bits and pieces, all the rubbish that shouldn't be in there, because that used to go for waste, it used to go for waste chocolate. I used to bring bags of it home for John! I should think I worked everywhere. There was another room, the Sorting Room. I used to go in there, and I used to have to lift them boxes, ooh it made my back ache: I was lifting big boxes of raisins off the belt and on to the platform. Sally, she was in charge of the Rolo Room. I liked her. And there was Mavis, and Polly, and Joan, they were all the charge hands, telling you if you were doing the job properly. They showed me what to do. They were quite good. Sometimes the girls used to hide my broom up for a joke. But that charge hand, Cissy, was horrible. Ann couldn't put up with her, and she went and reported her once. Oh! she upset me! In the Tank Room, she got onto me about the bowls, saying they weren't clean enough, but they were, they were! 'Look at them, they're disgusting! You've got no idea how to clean!' 'Don't you tell me what to do. I know how to do my job!' She was horrible, she really was.

We used to have a fortnight's holiday in August. We used to have days off. We went to France with Macintosh's. I went with some of the girls. We went in a coach and it was very good. We went to Paris. We walked about and had a meal, and saw the sights, the Eiffel Tower, Notre Dame.

And on a Friday or Saturday, in the evening, I used to go to that club that they used to have, the Social Club. We used to have discos, and I walked there from the hostel. It wasn't very far. I invited John (before we were married) to their Christmas parties. They were really good. There were a lot of people who I knew there, and a lot of the girls went there. Some of them, and the charge hands, came to our wedding! I liked the Social Club. You had to be a member. I was a member because I used to work there. They had Bingo, but I hate Bingo – I'd rather have a good old dance!

I had to go three or four months 'on the club', because I was ill because of worrying about John. He was ill and I was worried about him. I had all that worry. I didn't feel like going back. I couldn't face all that again. I didn't mind it, but there was going to come a time when I had to leave. I had loads to do here in my own flat. Work was important, really. I liked working, but there comes a time when you have to leave. So I went back to Macintosh's for a little while after that and then I left.

There were some bad times and there were some good times at Macintosh's. But you have to go through it. It was good having a full time job, but I thought about this flat – it wasn't getting tidied or anything, and you know, I had a lot of hard work really. I was at Macintosh's quite a long while. I left the hostel when I was 21; I worked at Macintosh's when I was in the hostel, and then when I lived in Morley Road, and then when I came here.

Own home
I left Macintosh's because I had so much work to do in this flat. I mean I never used to sit down. I used to come home, and I used to be washing, always doing something at night when I could have been doing it during the day. I like to keep this place clean, and then have my weekends free. John helps when he's here, but he's mainly out working. We have a big family who come and visit us here at weekends. After we were married we met up again with John's family, his father and brothers and sisters and uncle. And my brother visits too, as well as all our friends.

Conclusion

Why work was important
When you think about it, I wouldn't have never have got out, would I? Not really, if it weren't for work. I don't think the work in the hospital was fair. It was hard graft anyway, scrubbing here and scrubbing there. I liked working with the children, but I didn't like the scrubbing, didn't get paid for the scrubbing, that was really bad. Work was better when I left the hospital, because I was coming *out*. I was going *out* to jobs, that's what I wanted, to get away.

Why this chapter is important

It is important really because then I can tell people what jobs I've had in my life. I keep telling people, but they don't believe it, because they don't believe that I was ever put in a place like that. It's so people can understand what I've been doing. It has let people know what I've been doing in my life, and what I've been through and one thing and another, and just to let them know I've been pushed from pillar to post! I mean, that's the life we used to have. I try to make these people understand. Some people still say we need someone to look after us. They would learn something by this chapter, they would understand but now, they don't understand what a life we've had. They think when you've been in them sort of places you need someone to look after you but if we can manage on our own and come out in the community and things like that, they'll realize, well, they'll realize what we've been through. My message would be, that we don't need social workers any more, me and John. Some people don't understand what we've been through. They think we've had an easy life, but we haven't, we haven't had an easy life. I know what I put in my story is true, but it will shock some people who read it. That is important. I mean people think when you've been in them type of places, they think we're stupid, they think we don't know nothing, but we're not! I've got as much sense as anyone else. Just because I can't read or write very well, that don't stop me from doing things, do it? But people don't understand do they.

I think this chapter will help other people, won't it. I think so. Well, it'll help people like Julia. You know they're hoping to get Julia out. It'll help her. And I mean she's been here, she's seen my place, she knows what it's like. I want her to get out. I told her. She says she's going to try. She will soon learn. Cos I did. I felt ever so insecure. I just couldn't get used to it. But after a certain time, I did, though crossing all those bloomin' roads … Julia will know, if she read about my experiences.

You know who I'd really like to read my story? That's my old social worker. I'd love him to see it, I would. That would help him, help him to get people out. I just hope they get out same as I did, good luck to them. If he'd known about the crossing of the roads, he'd have helped me, but I kept it to myself.

Easy-to-read version

Chapter 4

Sexual abuse and women with learning disabilities

by 'Anastasia', Pam and Deborah with Michelle McCarthy

Four women wrote this chapter. Three had learning disabilities and one did not.

'Anastasia'

Debbie

They talked into a tape recorder, then later wrote down what they had said.

What is sexual abuse?

The women said 'sexual abuse' meant when somebody forced you or threatened you into sex. It could also be tricking you or bribing you into having sex.

Who does it?

The women said sexual abuse was mostly done by men. They thought men sexually abused women because they were brought up thinking they could get their own way. The women also said men abused and did crimes when they were drunk.

How do women feel?

When women are abused they can feel sad, frightened, angry, terrible. Women with children worry about what effect it might have on them.

Being believed

When women with learning disabilities say they have been abused, they are often not believed. Men with learning disabilities get believed more than women. The women thought this was wrong and not fair.

What staff do

The women said staff did not take it very seriously if they were abused by men with learning disabilities. The men might get told off but did not get taken to court or sent to prison.

The women said if a man with learning disabilities abuses a woman, one of these things should happen:

*   he should go to prison
*   he should go to a hostel or home just for men
*   he should go to a hospital
*   he should be made to live on his own.

How women try to keep safe

Some women do not go out on their own or in the dark. Some women wanted locks on their doors. The women thought if someone abused a woman, she should not go near them again.

Women should stand up for themselves. Say 'no' to men and shout at them if you have to.

The women said it was hard to be strong on your own. It was good to get help.

Women with learning disabilities can get help from:
- a worker
- an advocate or friend
- women's groups.

Messages for staff

Staff in learning disability services must take women's complaints and concerns seriously. Women want support from staff. Staff should know that sexual abuse is a big problem. Staff should help women to protect themselves

Staff should also help women with learning disabilities speak out about abuse and let people know what their lives are like.

Chapter 4

Sexual abuse and women with learning disabilities

by Michelle McCarthy, with 'Anastasia', Pam and Deborah

The authors[2]

Michelle McCarthy has worked with women with learning disabilities for many years around issues relating to sexuality and sexual abuse. Although she has written a lot about her work, this is her first collaborative writing project with women with learning disabilities.

'*Anastasia*', *Pam* and *Deborah* have been involved with the Powerhouse group for many years. Alongside their non-disabled supporters they have campaigned around issues on sexual abuse and were instrumental in setting up the only refuge specifically for women with learning disabilities escaping violence (Powerhouse 1996a and b).

'*Anastasia*':
I am disabled and I have learning difficulties.
I am a person who has fits and I have power to show my rights out.
To show everyone that I have the same ideas as they have, to do things for myself like anyone else.
I don't let other people take liberties on me because I'm disabled.
I fight for my rights all the time.
Showing my power out to let people know I can do things for myself.
When you go places and you're a person with sticks, people think you can't do anything for yourself.
I show I can do things for myself.
I feel good that I have the strength to show my rights out just like everybody else. I am a black woman with learning difficulties with a sight loss.

2 The women with learning disabilities chose to use pseudonyms or to use their first names only to protect their anonymity.

I am a black woman like any other black woman capable of doing things for myself just like anybody else.
All these things make me feel good about myself.
I've got rights and I feel good to support other people like myself.

Pam:
I am strong and powerful.
I've got my rights like everybody else.
I speak up for myself.
I like to talk with other women.
I do things for myself.
I'm going to get my own flat and share with a friend.
I go out when I want.
To do my jobs like everybody else.
I go to the pub.
I go with my friends like everybody else.
I like working on Powerhouse Management Committee.

WHY?
Because I am a woman with learning difficulties fighting for my rights like everybody else.

Deborah:
I am a white woman with learning difficulties, I am a woman, I've got a child and I'm deaf in one ear.
People call me names. I ignore them, I just keep walking down the street, I ignore them. I don't let them take advantage out of me.
I'm a very proud woman with learning difficulties.
I've done a lot of things for Powerhouse and other organisations for people with learning difficulties called Change and People First. We have good times in the Powerhouse. We have good laughs. I like that, I'm really happy when I come to the Powerhouse – I feel really good. I'd like to stay in the office all night sometimes instead of going home. We've been to Scarborough and so many conferences and training places. We've done so much, such a lot. It makes me feel good.

The writing process
This chapter is the result of a number of conversations between four women, three of whom have learning disabilities. All the conversations were taped, then transcribed by Michelle, who also edited them, adding some structure and contextualising comments and references. A draft

of the chapter was put on to tape for Anastasia, Pam and Deborah to listen to. They were then able to comment on it and thus also contribute to the editing process. When research findings on sexual abuse were discussed, Michelle presented these in as accessible a way as possible, including using pictorial forms to represent percentages (see p. 51 for examples).

The chapter is mostly in dialogue form, which readers may find a little difficult to get used to at first. However, this was felt to be the best way to capture the voices of the women with learning disabilities themselves.

Definitions of sexual and other abuse

Before any useful discussions about sexual abuse can take place, it is necessary to define what we mean by the term. Various researchers and practitioners have offered definitions, such as 'where sexual acts are performed on or with someone who is unwilling or unable to consent to those acts' (Brown and Turk 1992, p. 49) or 'any sexual contact which is unwanted and/or unenjoyed by one partner and is for the sexual gratification of the other' (McCarthy 1993, p. 282). For this book the women with learning disabilities defined abuse as 'all different things' (Anastasia); 'like hitting someone, or kicking them [shows bruises on her arm], that's what them men in my house done, hitting me' (Pam); 'thieving is abuse' (Anastasia); 'calling them names and racist abuse' (Anastasia).

They defined *sexual abuse* specifically as people being forced or threatened to do something sexual, for example: 'If the person says "I'll hit you if you don't do it" or "I'll kill you"' (Anastasia).

However, as well as threats or any other overtly hostile approach, the women were also very aware of the more manipulative ways people with learning disabilities can be bribed or persuaded against their better judgment to engage in sexual activity which they do not want. The following conversation demonstrates this:

Michelle   The other thing that happens is not threatening people with bad things, but bribing them into doing it, promising them nice things, like money or a present.

Anastasia   But that's how most people do things. When a man wants to talk to a person, he says, 'Will you have sex with me? I'll give you something,' that's what happens most.

Michelle   Do you know people who say that?

Anastasia   Plenty of people.

Michelle   Have they said that to you or other people?

Anastasia   I've seen it happening to other people and a few say it to me.

Michelle   Is it OK to try to bribe people into having sex?

Pam   If that happened to me, I'd say no. Some people do it in the day centres and group homes. If they do it me, I walk away.

Anastasia   They say, 'Do you want to lick me? I've got a nice taste.' They mean [points] their cock!

Michelle   So it's men saying this, is it?

Anastasia   Yes. Plenty of men around Newham say that.

Michelle   I dare say plenty of men in all sorts of places say it.

Anastasia   More in Newham!

It will already be apparent that the women spoke of perpetrators of sexual abuse as being exclusively male. Research and anecdotal evidence indicates that although not exclusively male, perpetrators are overwhelmingly male. Therefore, it is becoming increasingly common for commentators not to apologize for using the male pronoun when referring to perpetrators (Thompson and Brown 1997). However, these women with learning disabilities did not seem to be making a conscious choice to do this; rather they seemed initially not to be aware of the possibility of sexual abuse being perpetrated by women. It was outside their own experience and they had not heard others report it:

Michelle   You've all been talking about abuse by men and if we look at this picture [Figure 1] of my research, we can see that almost all (98 per cent) of the abusers were men. What this means is that sometimes (2 per cent) women do sexually abuse people. So it's not really right to say it's only men who do it, but it's only a small number of women and a big number of men.

Figure 1: Percentage of abusers who are men

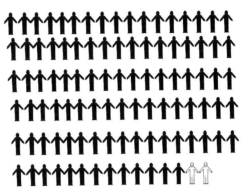

Deborah   I've never known of any women to do it, that's shocking.

A full discussion then took place about why it should be the case that that there is what others have referred to as a 'male monopoly' of sexual abuse (Finkelhor 1984, cited in Thompson and Brown 1997). The women with learning disabilities felt it was to do with differences in the way men and women were raised:

Michelle   Why is that it's mostly men who sexually abuse people and not women?

Pam   Men do it because they get angry.

Michelle   But women get angry too.

Pam   But men do the crime, like burgle people's houses.

Michelle   That's true, men do more crime generally.

Anastasia   It's to do with growing up and the atmosphere, a woman is more frightened to do more things than a boy is. Women don't do silly, nasty things, women got skills to do more of the important things than the silly things. Men grow up with the silly and dirty part in their lives.

Michelle   Often boys grow up learning that it's OK to treat women badly.

Anastasia   They grow up with the dirty parts and think they can do it on us, they think we've got the same feelings to do it with them.

The women accepted the view expressed by many feminists (for example, Radford et al. 1996) that the social construction of masculinity generally, and male heterosexuality specifically, led to the situation whereby boys and men grow up to think that if they want sex they can have it and if they want to push another person around in order to get sex, they can do that. Socially and culturally men have formed various practices which facilitate their perceived right of sexual access to women's bodies and the right to ignore the feelings and rights of women in relation to this (Kelly 1988, London Rape Crisis Centre 1988). The women could relate this to their own personal experiences:

Deborah   That's what happened to me with Joanne's [her daughter] father. I said to him 'No.' And I kept on saying 'No' to him and he forced me. I think some men can't control themselves properly and they should be able to.

Michelle   That's right, but the question is why don't men – or can't men – control themselves sexually? After all, women have sexual feelings too. Lots of women like sex and want to have sex … sex is not something that belongs to men. Women have sexual feelings too, but we don't let them get out of control and go around forcing ourselves on other people who aren't willing.

Deborah   That's right, I can control myself.

Accepting social construction theories of sexual abuse, inevitably leads to debates as to whether the propensity to abuse is an essential part of masculinity or whether, and if so how, some men escape their conditioning (Segal 1990). The women took very different views on this, with two forming the opinion that all men are potential abusers and one being clear that this was not so:

Anastasia   Every man is dirty!

Michelle	Is that true? Are all men like that? Do they all want to abuse women?
Anastasia	They all have the same dirtiness, but some have a lower standard.
Michelle	From what you're saying, it sounds like you don't have a very good opinion of men.
Anastasia	They all have the same thing in their heads.
Michelle	So do you think there are any nice men?
Anastasia	There's no nice men about. If they're nice for a few times, you always hear a nasty suggestion in the end.
Michelle	Does that mean you don't have any men friends?
Anastasia	They're nicer if you are a stronger woman, like a man. If they see you're harder, that you've got the energy to say things for yourself more ...
Michelle	Have you got brothers?
Anastasia	Three brothers.
Michelle	If you believe that all men are horrible to women, does that include your brothers or are they different?
Anastasia	They would say rude things to women.

However, Deborah felt this was not true of her experience: 'With the boyfriend I've got now, he doesn't do that kind of thing. There's a lot of difference between him and my ex-husband, a hell of a lot of difference.'

Michelle	Well, it's true that not all men are the same.
Pam	They *are* all the same. The men don't treat women nicely, men have got no manners. We are, we've got manners, men got no manners at all.

The consumption of alcohol has been linked to male criminal behaviour generally and to crimes of violence and sexual violence specifically (Brownmiller 1975). Once again this is something the women could relate to personally:

Deborah   Drinking is bad, because that's what happened to me. My ex-husband was drinking and coming home to abuse me, he hurt me and I ended up in a police van. When I came back I went to my mum's and I had to cover my eyes, I couldn't go down the road cos I had two black eyes and that is all because of a drinking problem.

The women's own responses to sexual abuse

The wide variety of responses that women generally, and women with learning disabilities specifically, experience as a result of being sexually abused is well documented in the literature (e.g. Kelly 1988, Kiehlbauch Cruz et al. 1988). In this small group of women who had come together on this occasion with the purpose of producing a book, there was an understandable reluctance to say anything too personal about their own feelings. However, one of the women specifically said she did want to record her experiences for others to read in the book:

Deborah   I would like to say something and I would like my ... thing to be put in a book, cos what happened here was ... I have been abused by Joanne's dad about five times. And when I went to the police, they took a statement and every-thing. I felt really terrible. I had to go to a Women's Aid place [a refuge for women escaping violent relationships] to stay in and I felt really terrible. I still feel terrible, I've got so much anger inside me.

Michelle   Well, that is maybe one thing it would be good to put in the book – what abuse makes women feel like – because that's something that doesn't get said very often in learning disability services and a lot of people don't realise how bad abuse really is.

Deborah   When I was abused, I felt really terrible, angry, and bitter.

Like other abused women (Ward 1995), she also worried about what effect living in an abusive household might have had on her child:

Deborah   Well, I can tell you this, I don't know but I'm thinking to myself if this is true and I said to my solicitor that Joanne's dad ... I was very frightened, because I kept on leaving her on her own with him and I kept on thinking is he going to do something to her ... because when he was living with me ... I get upset and I can end up in hospital thinking of this ... what he used to do when he was living with me and Joanne was only a little baby, he was naked every single time. I used to say to him, 'Put your dressing gown on, you can't go around naked, you're not in your own country to go around naked.' He didn't want to listen, so I'm thinking this in my head all the time and I'm telling my solicitor and she keeps saying, 'You've got to let him see her, you've got to,' and I keep on saying that if I let him see her, I've got to be sure that he doesn't abuse my daughter.

Michelle   Do you think they understand your concerns?

Deborah   The solicitor, to be honest, I don't think she's taken any notice about it. And now I've got a new boyfriend, who's going to come and live with me and he's going to be Joanne's stepfather and he would be very good. He was saying to me that I should let Joanne's father see her, as long as he don't start any trouble ... cos Joanne is in the middle all the time and I don't want that ... I've been told that she's a bit mad ... I don't think she is, but the school says she's been biting people and being aggressive to people, but she has not done that before and she's with foster parents now ... some foster parents can abuse children as well ... that's why I'm going to my solicitor next week to try to get her back and then me and her can go to counselling, so I don't end up having these bad attacks and end up in hospital again. Sometimes I have nightmares. Powerhouse has been helping me all the way, but they are a bit worried that it is going to happen again ... I was in hospital twice, I was under so much stress.

Being believed

Research evidence in two different countries covering a 10 year period suggests that there are high levels of disbelief when women with learning disabilities say they have been sexually abused. Interestingly, men with learning disabilities tend to be believed far more often than women when they report having been sexually abused (Hard and Plumb 1986, McCarthy and Thompson 1997). Staff and managers in learning disability services are often surprised and perplexed when they are presented with these statistics, not appreciating the underlying social attitudes which contribute to them. McCarthy and Thompson's (1997) view is that the high tolerance of abuse of women by men is a result of the widely held view that women frequently lie or exaggerate their abusive experiences. Also, homophobic attitudes can easily lead staff into very readily assuming that all or most sexual contact between men is abusive, hence the higher rates of believing men with learning disabilities.

When it comes to services, and indeed the criminal justice system, having to judge between what a woman says about her abuse and what the alleged perpetrator says, the women with learning disabilities were clear whose word usually carried more weight:

Anastasia   They believe the men.

Michelle   Why do men get believed more than women?

Anastasia   Because men say things in a stronger way than the way we do, they make a louder sound when they say out words.

Pam   I'll tell you something ... The managers don't listen to us. I got a lady manager and she don't listen to me. She don't listen to us and she don't know what abuse mean. I know, she don't. My family don't believe in it all.

Believing in each other and helping other abused women was a strong concern of this group, who had devoted much of their time and energies over a number of years on the Powerhouse campaign for a service especially for women with learning disabilities who had been abused (Powerhouse 1996a and b). The need for the women to organize themselves to do this was strong, as the response of the criminal justice system, and of learning disability services, is particularly weak when both the abused and abuser have learning disabilities, as is frequently the case (Brown et al. 1995, McCarthy and Thompson 1997).

Responding to sexual abuse
The lack of understanding women with learning disabilities often face when they experience sexual abuse and the consequent lack of appropriate

support has been shown by various research studies (McCarthy and Thompson 1997, Hard and Plumb 1986) and by ample anecdotal evidence (*Between Ourselves* video 1988, *Open To Abuse,* BBC2). The women in this group had strong feelings about this, partly based on their own experiences and partly on their knowledge of what had happened to other women with learning disabilities.

The women reported from their own experience that staff tended to tolerate high levels of abuse when it was perpetrated by men with learning disabilities:

Pam   I live with two men in the group home and this man hit me. I said to him, 'Excuse me, what do you think you're doing? What did you hit me for?' He hit my little friend there as well and she got a great big bruise, through him.

Michelle   What did the staff do about that?

Pam   The staff don't do anything. Carers don't do anything, key workers don't do anything, no-one in Newham does any thing. Then he hit the staff and the manager as well and my keyworker. The police came to talk to him and said, 'If you do it again, you'll be in prison and we'll get your mother involved.'

Michelle   And did that warning stop him?

Pam   No, he's carrying on again.

Michelle   And is he going to prison?

Pam   No, and he nearly hit the police when they talked to him.

The ineffectual nature of a 'soft' response by learning disability services and the police – often not recognized in the literature, and indeed actually recommended by some (Williams 1995) – leads to the situation where action is taken for the abused person, rather than the perpetrator:

Pam   That's what I'm moving out for, going to a new house in July. Where I'm moving to there's no men at all, all women.

Deborah   That's not fair, if it was me I would let him move out, not me. That's the way I would look at it.

Michelle   I agree, it does seem unfair that the person who has done something wrong stays where he is and the person who has done nothing wrong has to move out ... but I suppose what the staff might say is 'Where can we move him to?' If a man with learning disabilities abuses somebody in a group home or hostel and the staff move him, chances are he'll do it again in the new place. So I can see from their point of view that it is hard to know what to do with men who abuse.

Indeed, learning disability services are only lately beginning to grapple with this complex problem and recently some of the foremost researchers and practitioners have issued guidance to learning disability services as to what the appropriate responses are for men with learning disabilities who abuse others (Churchill et al. 1997, Thompson and Brown 1998).

The women with learning disabilities in this group came up with their own ideas:

Michelle   So if men with learning disabilities are sexually abusing women, where should they go? What is the best place for them?

Pam   A hostel for men.

Deborah   It's a difficult one to think of really, but I think just men on its own would be right.

Michelle   So are you saying that if men are abusing women, that they should be taken away from women?

Deborah   Yeah, put them in another place, in a hostel on its own.

Anastasia   Put them in prison.

Imprisoning men with learning disabilities has little support in the literature, largely because prison is considered an environment ill suited to anyone with a learning disability, not least because of the lack of support for their special needs and the risk of being bullied or attacked by other prisoners (Murphy 1997).

Michelle	Do you think men with learning disabilities ought to go to prison if they sexually abuse women?
Pam	Yeah.
Deborah	Yeah, I agree on that, definitely.
Michelle	Well they don't, on the whole, because people think it is not a good place for them.
Pam	They shouldn't listen to the men, should listen to the women.
Deborah	Put them in another place then, in a hostel on its own.
Michelle	I think that is probably a good idea, except then people would be worried that the men would probably abuse each other.
Deborah	Can that happen to men?
Michelle	Yes, it happens a lot.
Deborah	Really? I never heard that, that's the first time I heard that!
Michelle	If you look at these pictures from my research, [see Figs. 2 and 3], we can see that lots of women (61 per cent) with learning disabilities got abused, but also some men (25 per cent), though not as many.

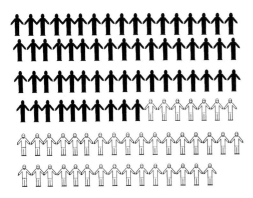

Figure 2
Percentage of women who were abused

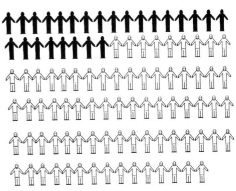

Figure 3
Percentage of men who were abused

Michelle	What do you think, Anastasia, should men who sexually abuse people with learning disabilities be punished?
Anastasia	Well they say that is against the law, but they don't do nothing to a person with learning disabilities abusing other people.
Michelle	They get away with it?
Anastasia	They do get away with it.
Michelle	Do you think people with learning disabilities ought to be punished by the law?
Anastasia	They should have the same punishment as other people without learning disabilities, or they think they can do anything, more than people without learning disabilities.
Michelle	Yes, I think that does happen sometimes.
Anastasia	They think they can get away with life easy, so they do it over and over with women.
Michelle	Is sending people to prison the only kind of punishment there is, or are there other things that can happen?
Pam	Talk to their family.
Michelle	Why would that be a punishment?
Pam	Because they should be put out of the home.
Michelle	Do you mean take them out of their group home for good?
Pam	Yes.
Michelle	And where should they go instead?
Anastasia	To a madhouse [laughs].
Michelle	What do you mean by madhouse?
Anastasia	They got a madhouse for people who can't stop hitting people and so on ... that is another kind of prison.
Michelle	Is there another word for madhouse? Do you mean like a hospital?

Anastasia	It's similar like a hospital and similar like a prison.
Michelle	Yes, you're absolutely right, that is what happens to people: they go to a hospital for people with learning disabilities or a secure hospital, where they can't get out. And they should get some treatment when they're there.
Anastasia	They should get more treatment in them places, because the welfare staff are more trained to keep an eye on them when they're doing the madness around the place.
Deborah	Or he should really be living in one of those places on his own.
Michelle	That's a very good idea ... so if a person with learning disabilities hurts other people, they should live by themselves.
Anastasia	They should have carers to help them do things on their own.
Michelle	I think that's a good idea, it means other people with learning disabilities are safe and they get the supervision and help they need from staff.

Prevention and protecting ourselves

Like many other women (Randall and Haskell 1995), the women with learning disabilities recognized that regardless of whether they personally had experienced sexual abuse or not, the threat or fear of it impacted on their lives in many ways. All had devised strategies for their own protection from men who they thought might pose a risk of sexual abuse, for example:

Pam	I don't go out in the dark, I'm too scared in the dark.
Deborah	When I get a mini-cab, I always sit in the back, because it's more safer than being in the front. And carrying a thing ... a personal alarm thing what I've got.
Pam	I don't go in the park.
Deborah	Women shouldn't walk in them places, like the park or woods or anything. If you walk in them places, you got to be aware, to look around you to see who's behind you. Like

I do if I get off the bus, I *always* look behind me, see who's around, then I keep on looking all the way.

Michelle   I'm certainly very aware like that at night when I'm out.

Deborah   And during the daytime as well. Once I was in a park with Joanne and I saw some guys ... and this happened during the daytime, and I had to say to Joanne, 'Pick up your ball' and I had to run from the park, so quick, because there was a gang of them and I thought they was coming to me and I had to run and Joanne was so upset and she was saying to me, 'Mummy, why are we running?'

Michelle   It sounds like from what we're saying that a lot of women spend a lot of their lives being frightened ... wondering who's around, where they can walk, where they can sit on a bus or in a cab. Do you think men live their lives like we do ... always looking around them, always checking who's there?

Deborah   No.

As well as dangers to women on the streets, these women with learning disabilities, like others (Walsall Women's Group 1994), recognized that they were also at risk from male violence in their homes:

Pam   Some men break in when you're asleep ... we got no locks on our doors.

Deborah   I've had to put lights and locks and a chain on my house because I'm frightened that men will break in the back way, over the garden.

These fears are potent enough for many women, even though they do not live with men. But there are added complexities when women are obliged to share learning disability services with men they are afraid of. Anecdotal and research evidence (Namdarkhan 1995) indicates that under these circumstances a kind of siege mentality can develop, with women with learning disabilities having to lock themselves in their bedrooms, for fear of male service users intruding into their private space and/or sexually abusing them. It is also important to bear in mind that 'mixed services' for people with learning disabilities, especially secure services or other challenging behaviour services, are often not genuinely mixed in terms of gender, but are often male dominated spaces with women very much in the minority (McCarthy, in press).

As with many other women, the steps women with learning disabilities took to protect themselves were generally those which, if effective at all, would only have been effective against sexual attacks from strangers. Despite at least two of the women having already experienced sexual and/or physical violence in their homes from known men, the women did not readily mention their fears in relation to this, nor come up with self-protection strategies. This is not something specific to having a learning disability; rather, it is a common phenomenon to many women and one which can be seen as a self-protection strategy in itself: if 'coping is defined as the actions taken to avoid or control distress' (Kelly 1988 p. 160) then focusing on the threats which come from strangers, rather than from intimate contacts, makes sense for women, even if it does overlook the reality of many of our lives (London Rape Crisis Centre 1988).

With regard to the sexual abuse that took place within intimate relationships, such as from boyfriends, the women with learning disabilities had what some would argue were simplistic understandings of protection strategies, for example:

Anastasia   Once a woman, a disability woman or not, has had bad things with a person, they would never go near to that person again.

This is clearly not the case for many people, so we discussed some of the constraints women might be under to continue contact with someone who was abusing her.

Michelle   Is it OK for a woman to agree to have sex with a man because she's frightened of him?

Anastasia   No!

Pam   She should go away from him, go in another room, lock the door, don't let him in. Men should put the little rubber thing on [points to groin]. They stop a woman getting pregnant and having sex with them. I've seen them.

Michelle   Yes, condoms are to stop pregnancy and diseases, but not to stop sex itself.

Pam	It stops that – not a nice word, not a nice word at all – getting AIDS, you can die with AIDS. It stops you getting pregnant, stops getting AIDS, stops a man from getting in bed with a woman.
Michelle	No, it doesn't stop people from having sex, it just stops pregnancy or diseases.

The need to be firm and assertive with men was emphasized by the women:

Anastasia	It's got to be the woman to stop a man from forcing you, you yourself got to walk away from the man and keep saying no, over and over, before a man can ever take notice of you. Shout it out ... with men you've got to really go for it, say words in a louder way.

They also clearly understood what could happen if a woman did assert herself (McCarthy 1998):

Michelle	What might men do if women stand up for themselves?
Pam	Hit her, abuse her.
Michelle	That could happen. Or he might leave her, go and find another girlfriend if this one won't do what he wants. And that's one of the things that women get worried about, is being left on their own, not having a boyfriend.
Anastasia	Not have a boyfriend no more! If you get away from one man, there's always plenty more coming around you ... when they see you on your own.
Michelle	Yes, it's true that people often get another chance, but that doesn't mean they don't feel upset when a relationship ends, even relationships where bad things have happened.
Pam	She should have an advocate or social worker to help her out.
Michelle	That's a good idea, sometimes it's too hard to do it on your own and you need help.
Anastasia	She would have another chance to get somebody better than him. I have had plenty of men asking me out. They say, 'Have you had sex before?'

Michelle	Do you mind them asking you that? It's a very private question.
Anastasia	I say, 'Why you want to know that for?' They say, 'You love me, can I have sex with you?' I say no.
Michelle	And how do they respond when you say no?
Anastasia	Put pressure on, so you say yes, keep trying. I say, 'I can't have sex. A person like me, a working person that's out so much, can't have sex.' The amount of things I have to do, being out and about, I don't have any time to have sex.
Michelle	What do they say to that?
Anastasia	They start laughing.

Messages for staff

We decided that we wanted to end the chapter by giving clear messages to those who worked in learning disability services. The women wanted the staff to take women's concerns and complaints about sexual abuse seriously and they wanted support from staff. The women thought staff needed help 'to be aware of sexual abuse, that it's a big problem' (Deborah). The women also wanted practical help from staff in learning how to protect themselves (Walsall Women's Group 1994):

Deborah	Defending ourselves ... I wouldn't mind learning that.
Michelle	Self defence?
Deborah	Yeah, that's what we should do, learn to go somewhere to do that ... I don't think a lot of people know about that.

The women wanted help from staff in speaking out about abuse:

Michelle	What can women with learning disabilities do about sexual abuse?
Pam	Put it in the newspapers, let them all read it all.
Anastasia	Make books about it, how disability people live.
Michelle	So is this book going to help let people know what things are like for women with learning disabilities?

Anastasia   Yes, from the past, how things was, to what things are now being a disability person. And making programmes about it ... what do you ever see on the tele much about a disability life? Nothing! We want tele programmes about what we have in our future, not just what you have in your future.

Part II

Fighting back

Introduced by Simone Aspis

'People are made up of three aspects of their life: emotional, physical and spiritual,' says 'Cindy'. The one very important dimension, which has been missing, is the political aspect of our lives. In my chapter in this section I argue very strongly that how we are able to conduct ourselves on a day by day basis is based both on our relationships on a personal and professional level, and on the rules, regulations and laws which govern our lives. The more one is unable to be economically active, the more these regulations will have adverse effects upon our lives. How much we recognize the importance of these social structures will determine how effectively we can fight back.

For many disabled people with learning difficulties, how they feel physically and mentally is important in their relationships, their participation in leisure activities, being a member of a group and being part of the work force. Disabled people with learning difficulties talk at length about issues which arise from their personal lives on a day to day basis. These issues arise every day whether that is safety, problems in shared living accommodation, having enough money in order to have a good standard of living, the pain and side effects of having inappropriate health treatments, support with mobility impairments, lack of appropriate support and accessible information. All these factors which are very real in the lives of disabled people with learning difficulties affect their self-esteem and the range of choices they have.

How we understand the personal experiences of our lives depends on how we view our disadvantage in society and what action is needed in order to fight back and seek justice. Most of the authors give their account of injustice on an individual basis without making the link with others with similar experiences as a way of explaining the injustice. They expect individual solutions often found within themselves and seek for equal relationships with professionals representing organisations who have power over groups of disabled people such as service providers, doctors, schools etc.

For example, Ros says, *'I am overweight and I want to eat a lot. I think I eat a lot because I get fed up. I suppose, not being able to get about I am going to see the dietician.'* The problem of being overweight arises from both a medical label and what the medical profession defines as not being some kind of 'ideal' weight. Ros was given tablets like me when she was denied the opportunity to get around the football pitch. When looking at weight we need to examine what is meant by an ideal weight and if there is such a definition. If so, is this a disregard for people with different shapes and sizes?

This is one example of how a medical approach has taken on our issues. By taking pills, somehow we will get slimmer. There's no regard for challenging this concept of height and weight and placing it in the context of the emotional and economic factors which affect our lives.

In all accounts authors explain the problem and the solution in terms of what they need to do rather than what's the problem in the economic system where there is a deliberate attempt to ensure that as many people who are disadvantaged are kept on low incomes via benefit regulations or being employed in unskilled jobs. As soon as benefit levels are raised, or wages of the unskilled workers are increased, there is a trickle up effect upon everyone else who wants to be paid more. This is bad news for companies whose main interest is to make profit and keep the capitalist system going. And raising benefits would act as a disincentive for everyone to be encouraged to seek low paid jobs.

This has become a very serious issue, as the request for long-term sickness and unemployment benefits has increased due to the decline of factory and labouring jobs, which disabled people with learning difficulties had traditionally undertaken. By examining the economic system, based on global market forces, we can start looking at poverty not in terms of cutting back or choosing between essential items and being careful with money and expectations, for all who wants work will find it. However, poverty would be examined as a negative side-effect of capitalism, which goes out to exploit and control the most disadvantaged people's life styles. Within a capitalist system poverty will always exist and those who are most affected will be those who are at the greatest disadvantage, such as disabled adults with learning difficulties. A successful capitalist system can never be run on full employment and generous benefits for those unable to work. Consequently, if we examine the economic system then we can look at what economic system would be required to ensure everyone can have access to a good standard of living.

In addition disabled people with learning difficulties are denied a high standard of living because all the women have attended special schools or have enrolled on courses for disabled people with learning difficulties. It is not expected that disabled young people will achieve much, so, therefore, they have a restricted curriculum and learning experiences on how to solve problems and make decisions in their own way. Most good jobs require people to think for themselves and make decisions. If school does not prepare young people to make decisions then how could disabled people with learning difficulties have opportunities for well paid employment if that is what is wanted? In schools there is some kind of expectation that disabled people with learning difficulties cannot think for themselves.

Decisions on who does not go to mainstream schools are done based on tests and exams, which everyone takes. Teachers, college lecturers, parents and educational psychologists are told that the person is slow or not normal and thereafter is labelled. There is some kind of idea of what is normal in terms of how people learn and what they should be able to do at different ages. Young people know that life is better if they are not labelled so the pressure is on them to conform and to continue to prove themselves.

Disabled people with learning difficulties are not supported to look at what they think the label is and where it comes from. By supporting disabled people with doing this would mean challenging the power of society through professionals who are paid to label and segregate people. How we understand what *learning difficulties* means determines where we see the problem. If we see learning difficulties as being people who are unable to do things then our action would be to ensure that they are taught to do so and can't move on to the next stage. The response would be either if a person could not achieve a given step then they can't go forward based on assumptions that there is only one way of accessing opportunities. However if we look at the learning difficulties label as a product from a system which thinks it's right to grade people according to some kind of normal standards then we are in a position to challenge the problem in society. In this case one would not be looking for individual but collective solutions and actions. When we start to see learning difficulties as a problem of non-disabled people thinking that everyone must be the same and learn in the same way then we can start to challenge people who want to keep on judging us and saying if we can have the same opportunities as everyone else.

When we do this then the problem must be put into society in terms of fighting for civil rights laws, and against local authority policies and institutional policies and regulations which restrict our opportunities. In order for this to happen, disabled people need a framework which explains how and why society discriminates against them. Without such a framework or philosophy disabled people will always be subject to the perpetuation of being trained to be acceptable disabled women, with this idea being defined by non-disabled men in western society.

Even when women meet together in women's groups there appears to be no collective examination of their issues. Women's groups are there to support individual women with finding individual solutions to their problems, which they experience on a day to day basis. The chapter by Eastleigh WILD in this section shows that on the whole they do not incorporate a political perspective on the lives of disabled women with learning difficulties, or when there is conflict in the existing feminist or political perspectives that women are encouraged to challenge this. It should be assumed that a women's group comes under a collective perspective with the assumption of using feminist philosophy as a basis to develop and extend the ideas so that disabled women with learning difficulties are better equipped to examine their mistreatment from their relationship with society. It's the same with mixed groups of disabled men and women with learning difficulties where not even a disability philosophy, such as the Social Model of Disability, is used to give them an understanding of their mistreatment as disabled people.

What is clear is that individuals and groups of disabled women with learning difficulties do not have the opportunities to develop ideas, which explain their discrimination and their relationships with other groups of people in society. Such a tool would need to be developed at a personal and collective level, which would enable us to understand the barriers which we face and explain how we would fight back. This would need to be developed through some groups of disabled people with learning difficulties. Thereafter we would need to be fighting for a fairer system which enables disabled people with learning difficulties to have access to the same opportunities for everyone by challenging society for upholding an economic system which makes sure that people who are tested for intellectual imperfections will be segregated and live in poverty, with little choice and lots of control over our lives.

In summary, fighting back means challenging services and professionals' organisations, local authority policies and government laws, which will have an effect upon how society organises its opportunities and support for people of different abilities.

Easy-to-read version

Chapter 5

A disabled woman with learning disabilities fights for her rights

by Simone Aspis

I went to Special School. I was labelled because professionals think children should perform in a set way at a set home at a given age.

I hated everything about it. The School thought we could not learn much.

There was no library.

The teachers had too much power. They bullied us.

I complained about my education to the Government. But I didn't understand the reply and did not know what to do next.

Even though new Acts have been passed, disabled children are not allowed to make decisions about their lives. Their parents make them.

The Special School system messed up my relationship with my family. My family sided with the Special School system.

My parents wanted me to be normal. They employed professionals to make me normal.

I had no personal space at home because I went to boarding school. My room was my dad's workroom.

I wanted to leave home. The only place I could go was a group home, but parents ran that too. I protested, but parents threatened me.

I was lucky, I got my own flat and now earn my own living. But most disabled people with learning difficulties cannot do that because Local Authorities won't pay for it.

My life changed when I got to be a trainee at the BBC. I worked on disability programmes. Then I joined People First as their campaigns worker. We campaigned for Direct Payments and Civil Rights.

Now I am campaigning to get the Education Law changed so that disabled children can challenge their parents' decision and have the right to go to a mainstream school.

Disabled people with learning difficulties need to join together to challenge the low value society places on us.

Chapter 5

A disabled woman with learning disabilities fights back for her rights

by Simone Aspis

Segregation for most disabled people with learning difficulties is life long and it starts right from birth until one dies. Well this could have been the case for me but fortunately somewhere and somehow I escaped this. I do not know how when no one wanted to listen to me. Actually, as soon as you are labelled as having learning difficulties it is assumed everyone knows better than you. So how are the decisions made about who has or has not got learning difficulties? It's simple, predictions; psychologists give you tests and if the test finds that you either perform tasks in a different way, outside the allotted time or age limits, then you are graded and labelled as having either profound, severe, moderate or mild or specific learning difficulties. Well it's the tests which examine whether a child can be taught in a standardized way that causes the classification, labelling and segregation of children. And this is particularly true with me.

I went through the whole special school provision right from the age of two until 16. I always remembered I hated everything about the special school system and everyone who was involved. This started when I was three when I used to attend physio sessions in the Finchley Road (London). My first direct action was kicking the physiotherapists while trying to run out of the therapy room and deliberately spilling yoghurt around the room when being forced to eat it in front of the mirror.

My rebellion was against the special school system. I found myself having a sub-standard education which was based on a curriculum with very few subjects. I never did subjects like biology, physics, science, geography and French and whatever we did was in the main repeated each year for new students. My curiosity for nature and science was not helped by a library of very few books, no newspapers and being in bed at early times which meant we missed many of the current affairs and science programmes.

Unfortunately, the National Curriculum, which all maintained schools must undertake, was not in place when I was a student. Even with inspections, I was never asked what I thought about the appalling standard of education I received.

What was worse than the sub-standard education was the emotional and physical bullying which went on among the students and staff alike. The headmaster would undermine the students' confidence and every mistake or murmur was a punishable offence. Even if a student did not like the same football team as the headmaster a punishment was dished out.

During the holidays I used to complain a lot about the school and my parents would report me for misbehaving. I would come back to school where the headmaster would dish out further punishment, which I never completed. One incident that stays in my mind today was when the head pushed me to the wall and grabbed me by the neck and threatened me if I call the school a prison. And, yes, it was like being in prison in every sense, silly routines of having to line up for everything including entering into buildings, on occasions in and outgoing letters were checked, phone calls were listened to, one was compelled to participate in activities and was force-fed. I was given appetite suppressants to help control my weight. I used to spit the pills out, which had resulted in much more subtle plans of pretending to swallow the pills in front of the head. I believed a healthy diet and a good game of football did the trick. Unfortunately, it is the parents and not children who could consent to treatment. This is wrong because it is the child who must undertake the medical treatment.

One needed to seek permission for every single move, whether that was to make a phone call on the school's premises, go in and watch television or play outside. I used to try and get my parents to sign a piece of paper and thereafter write a letter requesting that I would be taken out of the activities I did not want to participate in, like Girl Guides. One of the activities I enjoyed was when a friend and I had set the Dump Pupils to look at issues of segregation and to make up songs.

Unfortunately, groups of young people are still unable to function independently because funding can only be applied for if the group is constituted and, in most cases, registered as a charity. Under the Charity law trustees must be over 18 years of age, so this and the legal age when young people can earn money makes it difficult for young people to run groups independently of adults (including parents).

I never had the resources and support which some groups have, like the Young And Powerful, to run and support inclusive education campaigns. I could never see the resources coming from my parents or extended family! Actually my Grandma would much prefer to give donations to the school where I was emotionally and physically abused.

Anyway, with what few resources I did have I decided to see if the Secretary of State for Science and Education (Sir Keith Joseph) could assist after my complaints went unheard by the social workers and my parents. Sadly, I did not understand his reply and could not pursue my complaint further. Unfortunately, it was not helped by not knowing about the local authority role and policies and the 1981 Education Act.

In addition to disability rights, I had an interest in women's rights and equality issues. All over my wall were positive images of women pursuing men-type jobs and I was a big *Spare Rib* reader. I had a love for maths and decided to learn how to use a computer. Fortunately, my parents were granted permission by the professionals and this support was forthcoming. I went on a computer course during one of my summer holidays and loved it. Computer programming was the activity I felt I had control over. This was one area in my life I was being supported, to the extent that my dad gave me a personal computer which I used at school. Well, that was when the trouble began as the headmaster did not like the idea of women doing computers in the same way as he did not think football was appropriate. I wrote again to the Secretary of State for Science and Education under the 1975 Sex Discrimination Act as to whether schools can offer more favourable treatment for children of one sex to have access to a particular subject. In protest, I had an article published in the *Daily Mail* about the lack of involvement of young women in computers and designed some posters with a photo of myself (as role model) using a computer.

The school was either preparing us for a life in institutionalised care or low paid and low skilled jobs which require little else other than conformity and persistence. These were the roles which society expected the school students to have because we are labelled.

The government has passed the Human Rights Act, which incorporates the European Convention of Human Rights, which still gives parents, not the child, the right to make decisions about his/her education. What I was not aware of at that time was that the 1981 Education Act, which has been replaced by the 1996 Education Act and 1995 SEN Tribunal regulations, allowed parents to force their disabled children to attend a special school against their wishes. The Education law assumes that parents know best. It was the Education law which gave my parents power to force me to attend a special school against my wishes. Even after leaving the school, the 1986 Disabled Persons Act would not be of any assistance because there is no provision or recognition of independent advocacy for the disabled person (especially if under 18). And this is why I believe very strongly in the UN Declaration of Human Rights (Article 12) which says, 'Children have a right to a voice in all matters which concern them.' However, this needs to be extended so that all children must be able to make decisions on all matters relating to their life.

Segregation and the business of trying to make me normal did not stop at the school gates. During the holidays my parents had a line of professionals queuing up to see me and none of them had the guts to tell my parents, 'Listen to your daughter.' Am I surprised, when my parents were paying for their consultations and to confirm that I was the problem!

I was intrigued to know why I was the problem so I had my ear to the wall and bugged the family's phone to find out more. At the end of the day if the professionals told my parents that they should start listening to me then they risked not being paid by my parents. In addition, professionals need to protect not only their own jobs, but the jobs of their colleagues which have been created by the segregated system.

There was a glimmer of hope when my parents thought I could attend a mainstream school. However, this was short-lived when my parents allowed the educational psychologist to prevail over my parents' better judgement! The educational psychologist's argument for advising my parents to keep me at a special school was because I would be irritating for people with quicker brains. It was at this time when at long last I did start to experience some normal childhood where I travelled around independently with my friends and attended mainstream multi-activity programmes.

Even with the introduction of the 1989 Children Act, nothing would be any better as the local authority only has to take into account the young person's views. In other words, the young person cannot make decisions themselves. There is some protection afforded to young people in local authority care where they spend a great deal of their time out of their parents' home. I see being shoved away in a boarding school as like being in an alternative care system so, therefore, I should be afforded the same opportunity of making complaints to the local authority and having access to an independent visiting scheme.

Even after I had left the special school, the headmaster tried to gag me by instructing a school solicitor to write to me after a number of published articles. What is worse is that I know the head has threatened ex-pupils (aged 30) to keep away from me because I am trouble.

Well I exercised my right at 16 to leave that special school and return home. I was very clear I wanted to be at home and attend a college to undertake a Computer Studies course. Also I had applied to enrol on a Sunday morning Jewish Studies class and the head wanted me to attend a class with younger students because it was known that I had attended a special school.

Like being at school I felt I had no personal space at home. Because I was at boarding school and my parents were so used to me not being around for most of my childhood, part of my room was allocated for my dad's tools and this meant I could never guarantee any privacy and space to be alone with my feelings and thoughts. This intrusion was not only limited to the evenings but throughout the nights as my dad likes to do his odd jobs in the early hours in the morning. It almost felt that I was always a visitor rather than a member of the family.

After leaving school my parents hoped I was fashionable, ready to find a boyfriend and have some 'normal' friends. Well none of these happened as

I soon discovered that being a member of an integrated youth club was the last place for true inclusion. The integrated youth club had games in the gym, disability training based on simulation, and outings and holidays. What I soon discovered was that there were no two-way relationships between the disabled and non-disabled youngsters and that the sessions were mainly led by public and independent school students. I had conducted a survey asking young disabled people whether they had friends with the non-disabled people and did they see their friends outside the club's activity programmes and holidays. Instead of the Head of Youth being interested in my findings, he tore up my report in front of my parents and the social worker.

When looking back I had very little in common in relation to lifestyle and socialisation experiences. I realise an integrated youth club is no place to start making friends, especially where disability is not addressed at a political level. I wanted to apply for a youth worker's position and was told by the Head of Youth Services not to apply because all the children who attend the special school had a chip on their shoulders.

It did not take long before I realised that once a youngster had been sent to a special school then one is at a disadvantage by being labelled for life. Soon after I was nearly refused an application to attend an Israeli holiday, only because I went to a special school. Unfortunately, there was no anti-discrimination legislation which prohibited service providers, youth clubs and employers to treat disabled people less favourably.

I do not think that the Disability Discrimination Act would have made any difference because I would not be impaired enough, as the eligibility criteria is that the person's disability must affect his/her ability to carry out everyday activities. However, I do think we need anti-discrimination legislation which is based on the Social Model of Disability – the removing of social, economic, environmental and cultural barriers.

I continued studying Computer Studies at university. Soon after I decided not to pursue a computer career but move into the disability field. I had started working with the Special Olympics and helped the first disabled person with learning difficulties become professionally sponsored. This was the World Special Olympic Powerlifting Champion,

Gary Jelen. During my time with the Special Olympics, I had many arguments with my parents because they wanted me to have an Information Technology career. This was not helped when my mum accused me of not being able to get on with 'normal' people. Anyway, it was time to move on, but where to was the problem, especially without any paid work. Unfortunately, the only acceptable way was to move into a group home which was controlled in the main by the parents of the residents. At first it was great, but anything can be better than arguing over a disabled weightlifter on a day in and day out basis. Soon after I discovered what living in a group home was really like.

Support Tenants wanted to rule the roost and always wanted the upper hand. They had the cheek to try and set rules about what time visitors were asked to leave, visitors staying over night, telling us that we should eat and be together more as a group. Actually, originally tenants were not invited to the committee meetings which made decisions about the running of our homes and living conditions. Even with the rent, the parents, not the tenants, were first told about the rent hikes. I had gate-crashed a special executive meeting informing all the parents about the rent changes. My parents were embarrassed by my presence then, yet again they were equally unhappy about the complaints and information provided about my activities, which involved trying to secure better conditions with the other tenants. Like with the school, my parents decided to take sides with the group home because they feared me being chucked out. Indeed, my parents did not want to know when I was physically assaulted. Actually, my dad said I deserved it – this was even before hearing what had happened. What had happened was that all the parents stuck together and none of them wanted to support their children.

One support tenant put the fear into the tenants when she found out that I was working with them to organise a Tenants Association. This led to the support tenant in my house saying I had a chip on the shoulder because I always wanted to stick up for disabled people. The committee members left us living in sub-standard conditions where decor was poor, maintenance was not completed and complaints about the management were not taken seriously. In addition, for four years none of the tenants had a tenancy agreement, which made the business of who was accountable very fuzzy.

It was only by sheer chance while I was visiting someone else in his/her group home that I saw a Housing Corporation notice outlining what the Housing Association's duties were. Fortunately, I managed to pick up the 1985 Housing Association Act and Housing Corporation's policy, which outlined what all my rights were. However, the Housing Association should have ensured the organisation running the homes on behalf of them were running things properly.

Well, what I did get was letters from the parents threatening me that my letters were going to be examined by a lawyer. At this point I took the matter up with the Housing Association. During that time I was assaulted by another tenant and was physically threatened by his father if I pursued the complaint. There was no investigation. Over the coming months I collected all my evidence to support the parents' deliberate failings and presented my findings to the Housing Association. The report was used to make the Housing Association consider taking back the management of the house from the organisation. I soon discovered that living in a group home is like living in a long-stay hospital because of the imbalance of power between tenants/residents/patients and man-agement agents, service providers and hospital management boards. This is because these people have the budget and will make the major decisions on how the money will or will not be spent, the policies, rules and routines, and who will and will not be admitted. The fear of evic-tion is enough to make those who live in institutions conform to what was required of them and if they break loyalty all hell may be let loose. One AGM, which was the last one to which tenants were invited to, caused a real storm as I went 'public' about the complete mismanagement of the homes. I was ridiculed and told 'I was too intelligent for my own good'. Soon after the AGM one of the patients on the phone said 'I will kick you in the bollocks'.

Why are parents always involved in decisions about their children? I had parents of their children asking my parents if I would be willing to go out with them, why friendships were broken down and would I go on holiday. I even know one parent who had asked my parents if I would want to share a flat with their disabled youngster! Why on earth do parents still think they can make decisions about their child's life?

There is also an implied assumption that there are no different interests between carers/parents and their children. When looking at local authority policies on services for disabled people with learning difficulties, consultation with both carers and service users is expected. Services, I think, are designed to maintain protection and restriction, which parents and carers want so that they have peace of mind and, therefore, lessen the guilt if anything goes wrong. This is why mini institutions such as group homes and residential homes appear to be more attractive than direct payments for carers and parents. And this is no different between myself and my parents.

Well, fortunately I moved out and I am living on my own in a one bed-room spacious flat. For many disabled people with learning difficulties this would not be an option if local authorities are working within restricted budgets. Under the 1990 NHS and Community Care Act a disabled person would require a needs assessment before a service can be provided. However, the interpretation of needs may be different from the disabled person and the local authority. No disabled person I know asks to be put into a group home; usually that statement is 'I want to live in my own home'. The Lords' decision that the local authority does not have to provide a service if they are financially unable to do so will definitely mean an increase of institutionalised care for disabled people with learning difficulties. This will have consequences for disabled people with learning difficulties who may like to benefit from direct payments which allow them to live in their own homes with support. Unfortunately, the 1996 Community Care (Direct Payments) Act gives local authorities discretion on whether to provide direct payments and that it must be cost effective in its use.

I swiftly moved into the Disability movement via my interest in the Inclusive Education movement. My life really started to change for the better from then on. I landed myself with a BBC traineeship with the Disability Programme Units working on the TV *From the Edge* documentary programme and Radio 4's *Does He Take Sugar* programme. While at the BBC I became more involved with the Direct Action Network, who organised direct actions. As my contract came to an end, I decided I'd had enough of watching everyone else change the world and wanted to be part of the action. I then joined People First and became their Parliamentary and Campaigns Worker. It was here where my real politicisation process began, which was complemented with an advanced course in sociology. I oversaw the People First campaign for fully comprehensive civil rights legislation and direct payments for disabled people with learning difficulties. During that time I was asking myself what is speaking up and how do we go about it? Many people with learning difficulties think individuals make decisions and have the power. And to a certain extent this is true, but these individuals, whether civil servants, local authority or service providers, all have to follow legislation, policies and rules. Very few people with learning difficulties understand and appreciate the importance of such instruments. It's no accident that the segregated system and self-advocacy courses do not contain the importance of laws, policies and rules, because it is these instruments which will allow people with learning difficulties to see the conflict between themselves and the powerful establishments which still remain unchallenged.

And changes will be possible if all disabled people, including children with learning difficulties, are supported to have a voice and have lots of opportunities to influence decision makers. Legislators must build and develop an inclusive community.

Our biggest challenge must be to challenge laws which are based on society's values which underpin the needs of keeping a capitalist system running. We, therefore, must challenge people's worth on their productivity levels, economic worth and physical and intellectual ability to be economically independent from the state. For an inclusive society to exist we must abolish the assessment and testing systems which create the categories of people and pre-determine the level of segregation and control that a person must be subjected to by professionals and institutions alike.

We can do this now by sharing our political history and explaining to disabled children with learning difficulties about why the law is unfair for themselves and others and how they can become involved with the campaign for an inclusive community.

This would help these children's parents not to make the same mistakes as my parents and I can start doing this by being a positive strong role model!

I want to acknowledge that my parents did the best they could for me even though they were given appalling support by people who wanted to uphold the segregated system.

Easy-to-read version

Chapter 6

Good health?

by 'Ros' and 'Cindy' with Christine Nightingale

Ros

My name is Ros. I live alone in my own flat. I like living alone.

But I'd also like it if I could afford a taxi to visit friends.

I had a fall and now I can't walk far. I have to take tablets. They make me feel bad.

One doctor thought I had a certain condition. That worried me. I don't know what it means. He said I need 24 hour care. He wants me to leave my flat. I am very upset.

My advice is if you do not understand what the doctor says to you, get them to write it down so someone can explain to you.

Cindy
I am Cindy. I am 50 years old.

All my life I've been struggling against labels like learning disability. I have always been called a 'slow learner', or 'backward' or 'mild borderline'. I would like to be treated like anybody else, have a job, but I'm 50 now so where can I get a job?

I lived with my mum and step-dad all my life until 10 years ago when I decided to make it on my own. It was a shock to my system, I was so used to having someone else around to make the decisions. I still have trouble cooking on my own.

My real dad died before Christmas, I couldn't speak for three days. I was in deep shock. I still feel affected by my dad dying, it affects your emotions and your mental state. I was numb in my head, numb all over, sick to the stomach. I didn't go for help to a doctor. I am sure it would have helped.

My advice to health professionals is be more patient. Just let them talk.

My advice to people with learning difficulties is 'Go - they will listen to you.'

My advice to parents is let your children talk with the doctors and nurses.

Chapter 6

Good health?

Women from People First, with Christine Nightingale

Writing this chapter

Christine writes: Two women from People First, a voluntary sector self-advocacy organisation, and myself as supporter, met to write this chapter. Both women have an active role to play in the local branch of People First. Initially we all met together to discuss issues and plan how both stories were to be presented. Ros wanted to talk mostly about her physical problems and show how difficult it has been for her to be listened to. She also speaks of her fear of being diagnosed, at the age of 36, as having a genetically linked syndrome. Cindy, too, wanted to talk about her experiences of gaining physical health care. However, during the preparation of this chapter her father died. When Cindy and I met again Cindy decided to describe how her mental health was affected by her bereavement and how she found help and support.

Originally both women were named in the preparation of this chapter. However, fears that revealing their actual identities would cause difficulties in accessing services led to a decision to change names. They are proud of their links with People First and have used this organisation and the altered names for authorship purposes. Clearly both women could still be identified. However, we would all appreciate that their anonymity is respected.

Ros

My name is Ros. I am 36 years old. I have lived in this area all my life, first at home with my mum and dad until I was 21. Then I lived in various hostels. Eventually, I went to live in a supported group home. I used to fall down the stairs, so my room was in the dining-room downstairs. That was alright, we never ate in the dining-room because the tele was in the living-room. There was nowhere else to put me. I stayed eight years. I kept telling them I wanted to move. I had the doctor come in to see if I should move. I had to tell them my mobility was not as good as they thought it was. After a long wait I managed to get my own ground floor flat. I really like living alone, I don't get lonely, I can do what I want. There are people I could see who live across the city, but I don't have enough money for the taxi. I am very busy working for People First and have evening meetings to go to, and I see my boyfriend who lives in a group home as often as I can but I would like to see him more.

I am overweight. I know I shouldn't be this weight, it's bad for my legs. I have trouble with my mobility, I can't walk far and I can't manage the stairs. I have to walk with sticks. I have arthritis. It all started when I fell off the bus, about 12 years ago. I stepped off the bus and missed the curb and landed on my ankle. I managed to get to work at the training centre and I told them I felt bad and that I couldn't stand on me foot. They said, 'Right, you go up the hospital,' cos it was all swollen up. I said I can't walk to the hospital. 'Right,' they said, 'there is someone here with a car, they'll take you.' They thought my leg was broken but it was badly sprained. When you move it, it clicks. I couldn't stand on it. Some time after that they found I had arthritis. After the accident I had to sleep on the settee cos I couldn't get up the stairs. I think I might have it in my arms sometimes, they ache too. Before the accident I could walk from home to the city (about four kilometres); now the furthest I can walk is to the local shopping centre (500 metres). My life has changed since the fall. I haven't got so much movement, and I can't walk very far. The worst thing is not being able to get about as well as anyone else. I get fed up not being able to get about. If I could travel more I would go somewhere further than the seaside. I have been to London once on the mini-bus to campaign against the day care charges.

Now I have these tablets, I have a rotten time, they make me feel bad. I think they are too strong for me. I've only had them a fortnight, I feel half drunk. The last lot weren't strong enough. These make me feel sleepy. I am worried about talking to the doctor about them. I still need the tablets cos if I stand on my legs for quite a while it really plays up. I am worried that the doctor might change the dosage or the type.

Sometimes I have to see different doctors. That worries me. I sometimes don't know what they are on about half the time. I had to see a doctor about being overweight. He thought I had [named genetically linked syndrome]. I had to go and have tests. I had to go and see this doctor. He saw me on a video, I think, and he asked to see me. Me mum came with me, I think she understood. There was no one else there, just a student nurse. I don't know anything about this syndrome. They sent me a form, but I couldn't understand it, it was too small. I suppose I would like to know what it is, but I don't think I want to know what difference it will make to my life. I think he said it because I am overweight and I want to eat a lot. I think I eat a lot because I get fed up, I suppose, not being able to get about. I am going to see the dietician soon. I want to lose lots of weight. I am not sure what foods I should eat. If my transport gets paid for I will be able to afford salads and vegetables.

When the tests came back a doctor said I had a mild form of the syndrome. I still don't know what the syndrome means. I don't want it. When the doctor told me he sent my advocate out of the room, he then said that I can't look after myself and I need 24 hour care. He wants me to leave my flat. I am very upset.

My advice to health people and doctors is that they should take people with learning difficulties seriously. We can do what people think we can't do. People First have proved that. We run workshops, change leaflets and work with the police. My advice to people with learning difficulties on getting help from the doctor is: if you don't understand what they are on about get them to write it down so that someone else can explain it to you. Get someone else to phone and check.

Cindy
I am Cindy, and I am 50 years old. All my life I have been struggling against labels like learning disability.

Between 1953 and 1961 I went to the old open-air school. This meant they opened all the windows, except in the winter, and let you have fresh air and plenty of room. If you were a little bit slow, that's where they put you. They used to call people with learning difficulties 'backwards' in those days. I used to take the label in my stride in those days, to keep the peace. I didn't know what the word meant. A slow learner, that's what I was always called.

After school I went to workshops and things like that. There was nothing else to do, no-one would take you on. They were for people less able than I was so I had to conform to that because there was nothing else for me. I felt I was a little bit above everybody, cos I was only a 'mild border-line'. To this day that holds me back. I don't really know what border-line means. Sometimes I can be right and sometimes I can be slow. I don't know. They are words I never really understood, but I took them in my stride. I was never considered 'mentally handicapped'. Even the psychiatrist said I was not, just a little bit slow. It has held me back. They put you in one category and they expect you to be there, just because you are a little bit slow, or do things a little bit slow.

I am an unwaged person, I am not employed and I am not disabled enough to get benefits or go to the centres (Adult Training Centres). I would like to be treated like anybody else, have a job. But I am not, I'm quite a willing worker, willing to work, get out there and learn and still am. I am still trying to change my life as far as going to school to try and change things. I shall probably be there till I can't do it any more. I'm 50 now so where can I get a job? People don't want old people.

My mum and step-dad kept doing for me, which didn't help. I have never shied away from the community, my parents saw to that. 'Get out, do the best you can.' They didn't want me institutionalised. I lived with them all my life, until 10 years ago when I decided to make it on my own. I went to the hostel for short periods to see what it was like on my own. The social worker told me it would be a shock to my system, and it was. It was hard not to ask to go out, I was so used to having some-one else around, learning to make your own decisions. Then I went to a halfway house, with someone like a parent who made your meals for you. That was for three years, then I decided to go to the group home, where I am learning how to cook, cos I am still having trouble cooking on my own. I like to go to Burger King.

My real dad died just before Christmas. The shock changed things around. Nothing else matters, it eliminates everything else. The fact was I was in deep shock. I learnt to be lenient. I couldn't speak for three days. I forced myself off the chair, listened to music tapes; I would listen to the words and messages in the songs. I was in deep shock, like my head bursting open, my head actually ached, I felt I was numb, I felt like things were happening, frightening things, things falling off the walls.

You have to take things one step at a time. I have gone through the anger stage. They said I made a remarkable recovery because of the kind of person I was, determined. They say I am headstrong. It was good I am headstrong, it helped me get out of it. It was one strength I had. You learn about your strengths and weaknesses in yourself when you go through these things. What I didn't need was people who were negative, because people are vulnerable when they are going through bereavement. I felt I was vulnerable to all sorts of ideas, all sorts of people with ideas. Just because you have a learning difficulty doesn't mean you are not the same as anyone else with feelings, you have guilt and depression. And although I smile now, I still have setbacks.

People are made up of three aspects of their life: emotional, physical and spiritual. I am a Christian and have been in that circle all my life. It gave me support, which was great. I went to this place called The Edge, which is a Christian centre, for counselling, sometimes once or twice a week. I couldn't handle things. I couldn't handle anything. I used to be in the choir, I had to give that up because it was too heavy for me to handle.

If people with learning difficulties go through a bad phase with their mental health because of bereavement, they should let the grief happen, there is nothing wrong with going through pain. Get help by finding a trusted friend, a loving positive person, not a judgemental person, some people don't understand. Take your time. Have plenty of space. Set some things in your life to one side, you need to give your brain a holiday.

I still feel affected by my dad dying, it affects your emotions and mental state. I still get twinges. My physical health could have got worse, numb in your head, you're numb all over, you feel sick to your stomach, and your eyes don't focus very much. Usually I am a healthy person. I try to look after myself; if I need to go to the dentist I go, and if I have to go to a doctor I do. I didn't go for help to the doctor; I am sure they would have been sympathetic.

My advice to health professionals is to be more patient. Some people with learning difficulties will take longer than others. Some people may not understand what they have, some people might need support, some people need just to be able to tell just how they feel. Just let them talk, I'm sure they'll tell you how they feel the pain. They need very good listening skills. They should know about what people's needs are, if they need support groups, community nurses. I can speak for myself but others don't.

My advice to people with learning difficulties is, 'Go, they will listen to you.' You must give the doctors a chance and listen to what the doctors have to say. Both sides need listening skills. They may need someone to listen. Sometimes people with learning difficulties might be frightened of the doctor or nurse. Fear can be a thing.

My mum used to do it all for me. My mum used to explain what was wrong with me to the doctor. It was daft the doctor would explain to mum, and she didn't always understand. When you do it on your own it can be frightening. My advice to parents is let your children talk with the doctors and nurses, not have them sit outside the closed door. They should be treated as adults as well. They should be allowed to listen to the advice. Let them make the choice themselves, as well. Work with them.

Main Points

*   People with learning difficulties need good information, either in writing which is clear and printed large enough, or spoken to us, making sure we have time to think and understand.

*   We need time and patience.

*   We need to learn how, and be helped to talk to doctors and nurses and other health people.

*   We must be treated as adults.

Easy-to-read version

Chapter 7

Women's groups for women with learning difficulties

by Eastleigh WILD Group with Karyn Kirkpatrick

This chapter is about women's groups for women with learning difficulties.

We wanted to find out who these groups included – women with learning difficulties, women workers in services, academics, and all interested women. We also wanted to know if they were using ideas about feminism in their work. We called the groups WILD groups after a conference in London held in 1994.

Eastleigh WILD group contacted as many women's groups as they could find and asked them to fill in a questionnaire.

Who took part?
Thirteen groups in England took part.

These included an Asian women's group, a parents' group, a group of residents of a service and three college groups.

Why did the groups start?
Seven of the groups started because of a specific issue; for example, being parents.

Three groups began after going to the WILD conference in 1994 in London.

Two groups were very new.

Only one group, Camden WILD, had been going a long time, since 1989.

Who set the groups up?
Most groups were set up by paid workers, or women with learning difficulties with support from paid workers.

One group had been set up by a woman with learning difficulties alone.

We asked why do you come to the group?
People said they come to:

'have fun'

'better than stopping at home and getting bored'

'share problems'

'help each other'

'learn about things'

'speak up for others'.

We asked why do women want to get together?
Most people said 'to make friends' and 'to have a talk' and to be able to talk about problems in private.

Some groups said that women were better listeners.

One group said that 'men's problems are not the same as women's'.

One woman said that she thought 'we're better than men, much more power than men – that's what I think'.

We asked what is different in women-only groups?
Groups said that it was less embarrassing in women-only groups, they could talk about problems, men, sex.

Lots of groups said that 'men take over, they won't give you a chance to talk'.
One group said that women are more serious about the groups.

We asked what does your group do?

The groups do lots of talking about:

- rights
- how to complain
- health and hygiene
- sex and contraception
- feelings
- keeping safe.

Some groups also did things:

- making a magazine
- writing a play about famous women
- making easy-to-read leaflets with health promotions
- listening to speakers
- planning and holding workshops and Action Days.

We asked what does your group focus on?

Most of the groups said that they talked about things that affected all women and things that affect women with learning difficulties.

We asked about contact with other women's groups

Eight groups met up with other local women's groups.

We asked why meet with other groups?

All the groups said it was important to meet other people and find out what they were doing.

We wanted to know if the groups included all women. We found that:

- the groups were mainly women with learning difficulties
- women without learning difficulties were often supporters and not members of the groups
- groups for women without disabilities did not have much to do with these groups
- apart from the Asian women's group, black or Asian women were not mentioned
- many groups said they talked about relationships, sex and sexual health, but no group said that lesbians were included
- most groups did not have contact with other groups.

We concluded that:

- no money, transport problems and little information make it hard for the women to organise themselves and link up with others
- we need a WILD newsletter and a database to keep every group's address.

Even though the groups are all different, they have taken on similar aims and attitudes so that the spirit of WILD lives on.

Chapter 7

Women's groups for women with learning difficulties

by Eastleigh WILD group with Karyn Kirkpatrick

Karyn writes: This chapter examines the role of women's groups for women with learning difficulties. In the summer of 1994 nine women from Eastleigh Advocacy Group travelled to London to take part in the first Women in Learning Difficulties (WILD) conference. The conference brought together women with learning difficulties, women who worked in services with people with learning difficulties and women who teach and do research in universities. The aim of the conference was to encourage groups that included all women; it was hoped that WILD groups would be truly inclusive groups which looked at issues affecting all women linked by a common thread, i.e. that of learning difficulties, within a feminist framework.

On their return, the women from Eastleigh were keen to set up their own WILD group. One of the women, Elizabeth Niziolek, was instrumental in making this happen and six months later the WILD group had its first meeting. Eastleigh WILD group has attempted to hold to the ideals that they first encountered in London. However this has not been without difficulty. The mix of women has changed over time and the group is almost exclusively all women with learning difficulties. Introducing and discussing feminist concepts has challenged people, and for some members there is a great comfort in sticking to the tried and tested idea of a support group.

When Eastleigh WILD discussed ideas for this chapter, those members who had been to the London WILD Conference were keen to find out how the other groups were doing. The WILD Conference was a major event for the women who attended and is remembered and discussed often in the group. The group decided on sending out a questionnaire to as many groups as they could find. There is no central register of WILD groups and so contacts can be difficult to make. The members decided to send questionnaires to groups they knew already. They then phoned advocacy projects around the country, asking if they had, or knew of, any women's groups. In total 21 groups were contacted.

They then worked on the questionnaire. At a group meeting the members brainstormed what they would like to know about the other groups. A small group of members, Elizabeth Niziolek, Bernie Grace, Tracy Kelly and Claire Thompson, then worked on making the questions. This was the difficult part as we wanted to know whether the groups were following the ideals of WILD, but we also wanted to encourage groups to tell us about themselves, even if they were not groups for women with learning difficulties. It was decided to make the questions open so that the groups could write about all their activities.

The replies to the questionnaire came back slowly over several months. The replies generated a lot of discussion in the group, comparing the activities between the groups, and taking up new ideas. However, the most important effect of the replies was the excitement created by knowing that other women were also working together. Repeatedly there have been requests for another national conference.

This is not an exhaustive survey of women's groups for women with learning difficulties. Eastleigh WILD decided not to include groups set up by professionals to offer 'therapy' or short 'courses'. They decided to look at groups similar to themselves, focusing on all issues relevant to women with learning difficulties.

Results from the questionnaire

Who took part?
We received replies from 13 different groups, from nine areas. Walsall women's group runs three groups based at the College of Continuing Education, and there were three separate groups from Lambeth: a parents'

group, an Asian women's group and a group based in a women-only residential service.

The replies came from Camden and Lambeth in London; Swindon, Eastleigh and Bristol to the South and West of England; Walsall in the Midlands; and Wigan, Sunderland and Newcastle to the North of England. There were no replies to questionnaires sent to Scotland or Wales.

Why did the groups start?
Of the 13 groups that replied, seven of them were specific to an issue or a service.

Bristol -   women's health group

Lambeth -   Asian women's group
residents' group
parents' group

Walsall -   currently three college-based groups, begun from the Learning for Living Scheme at a hospital which then closed.

Of the other groups, three began as a response to the 1994 WILD conference in London (Wigan, Eastleigh and Newcastle). Two of the groups were fairly new; the group in Sunderland developed after hearing from other women's groups and Swindon People First developed its women's group after getting Lottery funding. Only Camden WILD had been in existence for any length of time, since 1989, and had recently received Lottery funding to expand its work.

Who set the groups up?
The following people set up the groups:

paid workers	6
women with learning difficulties alone	1
unpaid workers/academics	2
women with learning difficulties and paid workers	4
women with learning difficulties and unpaid workers	0

Two groups stated that women with learning difficulties became involved later.

How long have you been meeting?
The group from Camden had been meeting the longest, for nine years. The other groups had been meeting for less than four years, and four of those had only begun in the last year.

Why do you come to the group?
In all of the replies women reported that they went to the groups to get to know people. Many women spoke of their isolation and that coming to the group was 'better than stopping at home getting bored' or 'I enjoy other people's company because I live on my own'. One woman said that she went to the group 'cos I like the group … it's better than at home cos everyone listens to what I am saying'.

Other key reasons for going to the group were 'because women like to be helpful and share problems'; to help each other: 'I like it … to have the opportunities to help each other'; and to speak out.

Other reasons stated were more closely related to the purpose of the group: to learn about health; 'learn to look after our children'; 'find out about other women – famous ones'; 'to speak up for other residents'; talk about religion/culture; to 'tell services what women want'; and to organise Action Days.

Several groups referred to developing personal skills such as assertiveness, confidence and listening. Many women simply replied 'because I enjoy it'.

Why do you think women want to get together?
Again, most groups replied that they thought women wanted to get together to 'make friends, share things, have a bit of fun' and 'to have a talk – a chinwag together'.

For more than half of the groups it was important to be able to talk about problems and to talk in private, because 'you don't always want other people to hear things'. It was not clear whether talking in private meant away from men generally, from partners or from staff.

Discussing women's issues was mentioned by five of the groups, and several groups referred to sharing experiences and ideas and helping each other. Groups commented that women understood each other and were better at listening; 'with men we can't talk properly, no chance to talk. Men are always butting in or telling us to be quiet ... but it can also happen with women'.

One group pointed out that 'men's problems are not the same as women's, what concerns us does not concern them'.

None of the comments by women with learning difficulties referred to feeling 'safer' in a women's group, but this was mentioned by supporters. One woman commented that she thought 'we're better than men, much more power than men – that's what I think'.

What is different in women-only groups?
For two of the groups this was not an easy question to answer. The group based in a residential service spent most of their time in a women-only environment and the Asian women's group had been set up as the women were not able to take part in mixed groups.

The parents' group had been set up as a mixed group with a male and female supporter. However, they have never had any men attend the group – 'we don't think men are interested' – and the male supporter has since left. The group has not decided whether they would like to stay as a women-only group as not all of the group feels the same about it: 'we liked having a man as a supporter to the group, he was a very nice person'.

The other groups wrote that it was less embarrassing in a women-only group; they could have 'private discussion and discussion for women's benefit'.

The groups did not say what was embarrassing to them in a mixed group. However, they went on to mention the different subjects they talk about in a women-only group and this gives some indication: talking about problems, talking about men, sex, 'fashion and things'.

Comments were made on the impact of men in groups. Several groups commented that women talk one at a time and that men were aggressive and noisier: 'in mixed groups men take over, they won't give you a chance to talk. If you have something to say they take over anyway'; 'they tell you what to do, start shouting'.

One group commented that women take it more seriously. Another group said that they felt there were too many men in their services already, such as GPs, social workers and so on.

What does your group do?

All the groups gave a great deal of information about what they did; some groups described the way they organise their meetings while others listed their activities. There were common themes between all the groups, and it is possible to identify key areas of activity common to most groups:

- how the meetings are organised
- workshops
- conferences
- speakers
- topics for meetings
- finding money.

The groups reported a wide range of activities including topics for discussion. These included rights, complaints, coping with emergencies, feelings, keeping safe, self-defence, learning about food and diet, hygiene, sex and contraception: 'we did a project and talking about having babies, if we thought it a good idea or not ... not easy'.

The groups also did a number of practical things, such as:
- making a magazine
- writing a play about women in history
- developing accessible leaflets with a local Health Promotions Department
- listening to speakers on subjects as diverse as aromatherapy and the Greenham Women's Peace Camp; 'she had to go to prison cos she went on an army tank'.

Some groups got involved in planning and holding Action Days and workshops, for example:
- Camden WILD hold four action days a year; last year they were on transport and college.
- Eastleigh WILD hold a workshop annually to coincide with the local International Women's Day Festival. Subjects covered have been women and services, women and work, and parenting.

- Lambeth parents' groups have held a Parents' Day Conference.
- The group from Skills for People, Newcastle, have planned and run a ten day course called 'Healthy and Safe'.

Only one group, Camden WILD, has a full-time worker. This is reflected in the fact that it is the only group which reported that it was involved in User Forums in their area, feeding women's issues into the planning processes.

Who does your group focus on?

Three of the groups said they focused primarily on issues affecting women with learning difficulties.

Only one group stated that they focused on issues that affect all women.

All the other groups stated that they focused on issues affecting all women but in particular those affecting women with learning difficulties.

Contact with other women's groups

We asked the groups about their contacts with other women's groups. Eight groups replied that they had joined up with other groups, and five had not. Of the eight that had joined with other groups, three of them were all based at the same college and occasionally held joint activities.

Most contacts were with local groups. Four groups had contacts nationally, but no groups were in contact with international women's groups. Four groups had no contact with other women's groups.

Why meet with other groups?

Those groups who had contacts were very positive about the outcomes, listing benefits such as meeting other people and having fun: 'it was good to hear so many voices together – giving each other support ... hearing about what other groups had done'.

Few groups reported any negative aspects of these contacts. Those that did said 'the meeting was a one-off opportunity and there was no money for women to get there' and 'it was sad to hear the bad stories'.

A group of women who took part in an International Women's Day Festival Fashion Show experienced discrimination from some of the other participants: 'They left us out! Some of the women there didn't want us on the catwalk when they were doing it.'

How inclusive are these women's groups?

At the beginning of the chapter it was suggested that WILD groups would be inclusive of all women linked by the issues of learning difficulties and a feminist response to the silence of women's lives. The replies to the questionnaire indicate that this is a far more complex issue than first imagined.

Membership of the groups is dominated by women with learning difficulties. Jenny Morris (1991) argues that the fact that disability has not been integrated into feminist theory comes from the difficulties with the feminist premise that 'the personal is political'. 'Whilst it is valid that each woman begins from her personal experiences ... we must also recognise that our personal experiences are shaped by the culture with all its prejudices.'

Feminist assertion of what women have in common has been criticised as being a description of white middle-class women, ensuring that the experiences of other groups of women are treated as different (Spelman 1990). Feminist theory has been broadened to include race and class as central issues, whereas disability has been largely ignored or dismissed. This poses problems for WILD groups seeking to develop coalitions with other women's groups.

The questionnaires showed that all the groups discussed and worked on issues of personal importance to the women. It is vital to note the importance of the groups as providing women-only space within which to share experiences, raise consciousness and develop strategies as a first step in the struggle against oppression.

One then has to question the role of the women without learning difficulties within these groups. Is it a supportive role enabling women with learning difficulties to follow their own agenda, or are supporters sharing knowledge and experience leading to the development of political identity?

From the questionnaires it appears that while the women with learning difficulties set the agendas for their groups, they were limited in their choice of topics to their personal experiences. Even though we deliberately avoided women's groups set up as therapy or short courses, a great deal of the subject matter was similar, for example, sexual health, food and diet, safety, assertiveness.

The questionnaires also showed a certain degree of homogeneity. The Walsall women's group based at the college had separate groups for younger women and also 'women in their middle years'. However, the other groups gave no mention of age range. In the accounts of the groups' activities there is no mention, other than the Asian women's group, of black women, Asian women or any other reflection of our ethnic diversity. Heterosexuality was assumed and lesbian women were not mentioned at all. Issues of concern to older women or young women were not specified. It is important to note that the different forms of oppression may well impact in different ways on different women (Williams 1989).

The further development of the WILD movement is essential to the progress of women's groups. Without the discussion and promotion of a feminist perspective to the lives of women with learning difficulties, women will not have the tools necessary to challenge their oppression, and will face perpetual 'training' on how to be acceptable women. As the supporter of the residents' group notes: 'We haven't spent lots of time on women's issues – more on issues in their lives as residents. It's something I will suggest – the women are enthusiastic.' Introducing feminism is not without its difficulties; the challenge lies in confronting the conflicts between disabled and non-disabled feminists on issues such as abortion, 'allowing' disabled babies to die, and community care. Addressing these issues can be uncomfortable for all concerned.

Of major concern is the isolation of the groups. There is a great wealth of enthusiasm, experience and commitment from the women involved which is hampered by poverty, access difficulties and lack of information. Overwhelmingly, the message from the women was the need to network, to make links and to learn from each other. A national WILD newsletter would enable the work of the groups to be promoted, to raise consciousness and to encourage groups and supporters to broaden their understanding of the sources of their oppression.

In gathering the information for this chapter, Eastleigh WILD tracked down other women's groups. Having identified the 13 groups involved in the chapter there is now the potential to campaign for a national WILD newsletter and database. Despite the lack of resources and the isolation of the groups, the idea of WILD has survived. The groups, while being individual, have taken on very similar aims and attitudes. The spirit of WILD lives on.

The groups who were involved
WILD Eastleigh Advocacy Project
Residents' Group, Lambeth
Walsall Women's Group
WILD Women of Wigan
WILD in Camden
Asian Women's Group, Lambeth

Sunderland Women's Group
Swindon People First
Parents' Group, Lambeth
Skills for People, Newcastle-upon-Tyne
Woman to Woman, Bristol

List of women involved
Mary Davis
Bernie Grace
Sarah Humby
Michaela Jackson
Lisa Jeffries
Tracy Kelly
Karyn Kirkpatrick
Sue Lamb
Carol Murphy
Elizabeth Niziolek
Maggie Parker
Claire Thompson
Zena Woods

Part III

Identity

Introduced by Sheena Rolph

Recent discussions among some professionals relate to what are seen as identity issues for people with learning difficulties. Some writers feel that many people with learning difficulties either are unaware of or deny the issues surrounding the label 'learning difficulties' and are therefore 'invisible to themselves' (Rapley et al. 1998). Several of the chapters in this book make timely contributions to the debate by discussing the way the authors see themselves and describing the experiences in their lives that have either undermined or changed and revived their self-image. I will draw out this theme from the five chapters in this section: 'My life' by 'Alice in Wonderland'; 'Opening doors' by Mina, Hilary, Marian and Jeannette; 'Rose MacDonald' by Annemarie and Rose MacDonald; 'You have to be strong for your kids and strong for yourself' by Sharon Bradley and Christine Marsden; and 'Croydon lives' by Mabel Cooper, Gloria Ferris and Mary Coventry.

In 'My life', 'Alice' describes the struggle she has had to maintain a sense of herself in the face of name-calling and bullying both at school and at home. She says, 'They call me mad ... blame me for everything that goes on in a day's time,' and she lists the abusive and demeaning names she has been called. Beneath this list of 'What they say about me', however, she writes a much longer list – 'What I say about me', which reveals her determination to maintain a sense of her own worth and to value her achievements. 'What I do in a day now is different, more control than in the school time,' she says. She takes pride in her sponsored run, which she undertook with two sticks but 'threw one half away in the middle of it'; in her appearance on TV and in the group she runs for black and Asian women. She describes herself as 'a very responsible person' in spite of the criticism she receives, and also a caring person who 'understands how to take headaches and pains away ... take stress away'. 'Alice's' story reveals that she is fully aware of her disability and of the stigma attached to it. She is not attempting to be 'invisible', or to deny it, but to be defiant, to change her life, and retain and build a strong identity despite the challenges: 'I know a lot in a day's time to what she (Mum) thought ...'

'Opening Doors' was a programme specifically set up to enable people to get jobs. Mina, Hilary and Marian describe the way their lives changed as a result of taking part. All three felt they had gained in self-esteem as well as in skills. As Hilary said, 'People keep putting me down saying I can't do it, but I can – which I've proved.' She felt she had gained a new identity through an opportunity which had previously been closed to her: 'It feels funny (being staff), you're the teacher to them instead of the other way round. It feels funny but good.' Mina also enjoyed her new role of public speaking, and her success in gaining a certificate at the end of the college course, and Marian felt 'really proud that I'd got something'.

Perhaps one of most significant aspects of this chapter is the way the women felt they gained a new identity through doing the course with women without learning difficulties. All three come back to this theme several times, indicating that they enjoyed the inclusiveness of the course, which enabled them to learn about the things all the women had in common. Hilary sums it up when she says, 'It has been different for me because I didn't used to mix with people who haven't got learning disabilities. I've always been to college with people with learning disabilities not without and I find that [i.e. Opening Doors] very good, very helpful.' All three women now see themselves in the job market, and have ambitions to get either paid or voluntary work, hoping to set up their own collective.

In Annemarie's chapter about her daughter Rose, she raises some of the problems the family have experienced at Rose's school. These have focused on the theme of identity, and in this case, some of the negative issues experienced in a mainstream school. Rose's teachers sometimes only see her disability and make incorrect assumptions about her lack of ability to take part in the more exciting or taxing aspects of school life. Annemarie outlines the difficulties of enabling Rose, too, to have an understanding of her disability. Far from hiding the nature and name of her disability from Rose, which is what some researchers have suspected happens in many families (see, for example, Rapley et al. 1998) Annemarie has told Rose that she has Down's syndrome, and Rose, though at first denying the term, now acknowledges it and uses it in relation to herself. Rose's sense of her own identity is affected by this knowledge.

Annemarie says that 'she certainly has a sense of herself as different from other children ... I think this affects her confidence in herself'. On the other hand, Annemarie provides evidence of Rose's strong personality, and her own taste in books, clothes, and music. When Rose writes about herself she is very positive about her appearance and about her life at home and at school. She says, 'I have got Down's syndrome. I don't know what it is. I think I look nice,' and she confirms her self-image with a lively painting of herself, smiling and active. This positive self-image is underlined in a postscript by Annemarie which gives an idea of the excitement Rose is now experiencing at growing up, moving to secondary school, and exploring a new life.

In their chapter, Sharon and Chris do not dwell on their learning difficulties. They describe what it is like to be a mother. Sharon highlights the difficulties of dealing on her own, or with the support of her family, with childhood illnesses and the relentlessness of the daily routine. She also feels that there are compensations to the job of being a Mum and takes delight in the companionship of her children. In the worst times, she sees herself as having the strength to manage. As she says of this difficult role, 'You have to be strong for the kids and strong for yourself.' Chris has the role of wife as well as mother. She has support from parent support workers and from her family to help her with problems. She, too, is positive about her role as mother, summing up her feelings by saying, 'If I was asked about what it's like to be a Mum, I'd say go for it.'

Mabel Cooper, who tells her story first in 'Croydon lives', expresses the purpose of her research as 'the quest to find out'. She had written part of her autobiography previously (Cooper 1997) but there were still gaps in her story and she set out to find out more about her life, her family, and her identity. By discovering details about her early childhood, her mother, the reasons she went into St. Lawrence's Hospital, and by discovering a family she didn't know existed, Mabel gained a new sense of who she was: 'It helps you in understanding yourself a lot more.' She had to deal with the knowledge that in the past others had given her mother and herself another identity, but she shows how she came to terms with the hurtful labels and definitions, as 'Alice' had also had to do, though in quite different circumstances, in the community and among her family. Mabel is quite clear that she would 'rather know than not know' as she pieces together all the hidden aspects of her life. Her experiences in the Record Office have meant that a new autobiography is emerging, as slowly 'it came back to me that I had people, a family'. This chapter has also given Mabel the opportunity to describe her many achievements since she left St. Lawrence's, all of which have proved the labels and definitions she was given in the hospital to have been wrong. As she says, 'A lot of things have happened in my life, but I'm who I am. I'll always be what I am, always!'

Mabel's friend Gloria defines her role in life as the carer and advocate of her friend Muriel. Her story describes how it was possible for her, in St. Lawrence's Hospital, to build this role for herself, how it is her continuing purpose in life, and has been for over forty years. As was so common in the large institutions, Gloria worked hard in the wards, in particular with the people with the most severe difficulties. Very often it was not easy for the 'ward workers' to establish long term relationships with any of the people they worked with, as jobs and people changed regularly (see Jean's chapter), but Gloria and Muriel were able to stay together and Gloria's help was undoubtedly much appreciated by staff. Gloria became, in effect, a nurse. As she put it, 'I worked with the nurses. Although I wasn't a nurse, I helped out and I quite enjoyed it. I loved it.' Like Mabel, Gloria is clear about her achievements and her role, seeing this role as being very closely connected with her past, recognising all the injustices, but maintaining her identity as friend and then advocate of Muriel as the one constant throughout all the changes. When she describes her work with Muriel, she says: 'It's what I like doing ... It's what I am.' She also recognises the mutuality of the relationship: 'I'm her lifeline and she's mine, more or less.'

In contrast to Mabel and Gloria, Mary has lived with her family most of her life. She sees herself as part of the family and takes pleasure in the fact that she takes after her mother, and looks like her. She is aware, however, of her learning disability and describes her time at a special school, and her difficult transition from family home to a group home. She is proud of her new life in her bed-sitting room with all her own things about her, and also of the fact that she now has a job as Secretary of People First, Croydon.

What emerges from all these very different chapters, is neither a lack of awareness on the part of the women with learning difficulties, nor a desire to be invisible, but an engagement with the fact of being perceived, either in the past or in the present, as having learning difficulties, great enjoyment of and pride in achievements and new roles more recently attained, and determined efforts to sustain and declare an individual sense of identity, sometimes against great odds.

Easy-to-read version

Chapter 8

My life

by 'Alice in Wonderland' with Jan Walmsley

My life has been bad luck from young to since school time. Something fell in my eye. Fits. In the West Indies Land I broke a leg, they didn't have the equipment and nothing ever happened. I got sickle cell.

My family

I got three brothers and four sisters. They call me mad. Blame me for everything that goes on.

My mum

Throw my mum in the dustbin if you like. I'm for ever out, going places out of her sight.

School

When I was at school as soon as they see me the only person walking on the road they took the mickey, pushing me all about the roads, starting from the kids and grown ups, the younger ones encouraging the older ones like a partnership.

What I say about Me

I done plenty of things. A big fat sponsored run in a church, I've made a television programme, I've been in a magazine, I run a group for black and Asian women. I tell my mum all these things.

Chapter 8

Alice in Wonderland: My life

'Alice' with Jan Walmsley

Introduction

Jan writes: I knew 'Alice' quite well before I asked her for her story so we did not need a 'getting to know you' period. I went to her to ask her about her school days, but in fact she told me a lot more about her life, especially how she feels about her family. We taped the discussion, and later I went back to Alice with the typed up story and a taped version. Alice can't read very well so she preferred to listen to the taped version. I stopped the tape after each section and Alice talked a little more about her story, which I added in.

I then asked her what she would like to be called. She immediately said 'Alice in Wonderland', so that's the name we've used.

Later she told me what she wanted people to learn from her chapter. What she said is added to the end.

Alice in Wonderland: My life

What I have done in school right up to what I do now, it makes a poem, like a rhyme, it's like a story.

How I got to be disabled
No definitely not born with nothing. Bad luck from young to since school time.

That's the first thing, my eye. Something fell in my eye.

Lead poison, that was the fits, lead poison, by just silly things. I never been able to do anything in school really because the teachers never know what to do about me in the schooldays. When I was in the school days, I used to have more fits than I do now. Because everything blamed on me, more and more fits every minute of the day, worse every day, banging and kicking. I don't hardly have it now because I am doing more things. What I do in a day now is different, more control than in the school time.

My legs, that was an accident when we been to stay in the West Indies. We been to stay all of us, the West Indies land, Guyana. I broke a leg, they didn't have the equipment and nothing ever happened. As soon as I went there to stay I stopped having fits when I was younger. It was only when I come back here I started back on the fits. That is what I notice, that fits is to do with what your control is in your life, so it's what is going on, that is what I notice from my own person.

Sickle cell. I got sickle cell. I am the trait, the bad person. I get ill easy than all the others, and any time I fall in a day's time, and any bruise it takes months to go away, so I get ill easy, everything what happens in a day's time. It all rhymes together.

I had a wheelchair and a three wheel bicycle and take it in different turns racing with a bike, a big fat bike. Having to use the middle of the road like a car. My mum break it up and dump in the back yard so it's all rusty.

My family

I got three brothers and four sisters. Eight of us. My dad died. He died when he was 58. He never even had his old age pension. Because he got bad, his liver, lots of poison in him. He never went to the pub, never a drinker. Sickle cell, when you got sickle cell anything can happen, in a day's time.

They call me mad. My family showing off theirselves, they're better than me. Blame me for everything that goes on in a day's time. My mum puts things in a place, she doesn't remember what she does in a day's time, so everything is missing, all the blame is *Alice took it*. And when she finds it, laughs her head off and turns away, don't apologise to nothing. Like this morning, my nephew threw the glass in the bin because he was upset at himself. *It's Alice, Alice done it*. And my sisters used to do the tricks. When my mum hide the food away, she doesn't want it to be touched, my brothers used to pinch it away and everything went missing in a day's time. *Oh look, it's Alice, look it's Alice*, blame for everything in a day's time, so everything is missing, all the blame is Alice tooken it. I used to have all the canes, all the hitting with the shoes, my mum, all the lashing on Alice's bottom. Everything has to be Alice, it has to be Alice.

My mum

Throw my mum in the dustbin if you like. Everything what she does is talk talk talk. I'm a sick person, I can't do nothing, I'm a crippled person. Just call me back a cripple, a dirty crippled tramp that doesn't even wash herself. How she tell if I wash, she never in when I am in, so how could she tell if I wash. I hide myself away, I only do it when she gone away. We creep out the door like two little creatures, one creature with a stick, one creature without a stick like creepy crawlies, sounds like creepy crawlies.

She lonely without me? No way. She can't be lonely without me I'm never in. She doesn't like she ever takes any notice, I am never in the house. I'm forever out, going places be out of her sight. To get rid of her screaming and shouting. I have been far away in the late night, stayed around with a friend, and she didn't notice, no.

I have got another sick sister who needs more. I don't show at all now that I am the disability person in my family. In the end I have to leave home because my mum is sick and got her own self, she needs to be more concerned herself because she sick herself with kidney problems, and got to look after my sister, Marcie. Her body burst inside of her last year. She have to be in hospital all the time and two of her kids with the welfare, so she needs more help than whatever I need.

She doesn't see it as that. They still act like I am the most unhelpful one. I got no sickness in the whole Wonderland family, and they always describe I am the sick one.

School

When I was at school everyone was worse around the 'Tinning Town' area. This whole area was bad. As soon as they see me, the only person walking on the road they took the mickey, pushing me all about the road, starting from the kids and grown ups, the younger ones encouraging the older ones like a partnership. When they see me getting a bit stronger, walking faster and faster, then they start encouraging more of each other. That's why I started with my sticks, cos I was a person with a wheelchair. When I start getting more active and more responsible, they start getting more frightened of me.

At school the staff used to just laugh and encourage the members, nobody ever took anything seriously at Lady Wedgwood School. I had to get confirmed in it by myself and have a word with my sister and just run about the school myself and run to Southleigh School next door, and they used to have the same problems, every one of the Wonderland family.

Everyone used to call me Alice in Wonderland. In the school times too I used to be called Ali Baba and the forty feet, then there was someone who was called Ali Baba in the same class they start calling me Alice in Wonderland. Because I am like a Wonderland.

The only person with fits, the only person with a blind eye, my eyesight everybody looks at. They used to take the mickey, even though it was a disability school and supposed to be a Christian school.

It all rhymes, school time to this time, because I was doing the same thing as training in school I'm doing training now the same thing as what I did in school. I see myself as a person training the teachers and welfare in disability things because I was the only one with bad eyesight. And I see myself today, the same what I were saying in school time.

What they say about me
Black Wog
Cripple
You're 'andicap, you can't do anything. You're cripple
You're mad

What I say about me
Crippled person all round the whole of Britain. I done plenty of things, a crippled person do whatever in a day's time. That is what I did say to my mum. She didn't know what to say.

I got more energy to move myself about than Marcia, than all of them in a day's time. A big fat sponsored run I done in a church, and demanding the most money. Sponsored run with two sticks, and throw one half away in the middle of it, I done well than all of them, got more money for the church that Christmas time. I've made a television programme, I've been in a magazine, I run a group for black and Asian women.

When my mum sees I am a very responsible person, that I know a lot in a day's time to what she thought. She was surprised to ever see that I am a person understands how to take headaches and pains away, take stress away. I tell her all these things.

Messages
For women with learning disabilities who read this:

Your parents: If your parents is not doing the right things you don't need to take it as it is. It's up to you in life. You have got a choice. You need to choose what you think is best for yourself.

Name calling: You can't really do anything about that. Keep yourself away from them by not encouraging them to mess with you. You just let it go on, it would go on for ever.

For parents:
Your parents must take the rights in letting disability members get

their point of view. They are not a stupid person to what you think they are, just because you don't hear a person do something, doesn't mean anything. They still got a brain in same way.

Easy-to-read version

Opening Doors

Mina Turfkruyer, Hilary Cooke, Marian Bridges and
Jeannette Karger, with Deanne Bell

The short story

Opening Doors was a course helping women to move on, to
get a job. The women learned about helping people with
learning disabilities who had been treated badly and abused.

There were nine women on Opening Doors; some of them had not got learning disabilities and some of them did. The women that did were Marian, Hilary and Mina. Deanne has helped in writing the chapter.

There was a tape to help us and a form and a meeting where we talked about Opening Doors and were interviewed, which was nerve-racking.

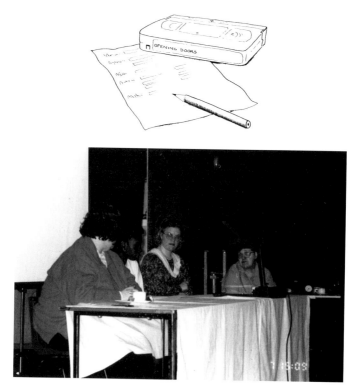

One of the interviewers was Jeanette. She is a woman with learning disabilities. She was there to interview us and she got paid.

Each week we got our programme. We went to work on Tuesdays – at places where there were people with learning disabilities and at places where people stay if they have been abused – refuges.

Wednesdays we had some people come into the classroom to talk to us. They did stuff like First Aid, we watched videos, we did Signing and learnt about learning disability people.

Thursdays we went to Cambridge College and we did lessons. We learnt about people dying and what it is like being upset and losing things like friends and homes.

We also did homework.

We went on stage and talked about what we were doing. We went to the Playhouse in Harlow to talk to women who work in refuges and to day centres. We also went to London, to parties and meetings with Powerhouse (a women's self-advocacy group).

To help us to get a job we got a certificate. To get the certificate we had to do work at home and take it in to Cambridge. It was looked at and they let us know if we'd passed or not.

We also got a certificate at the end of Opening Doors from an important man. Everybody was there from work-experience, Cambridge and people from the newspaper. We all had a photograph taken and it was in the paper.

The women feel they have got a lot from being on the Opening Doors course, like confidence and learning to go back to work.

Opening Doors was for people with learning disabilities and people without learning disabilities, which was a good thing. We enjoyed being together. We made friends. The women without learning disabilities learnt a lot about people being disabled. They learnt a lot from the women with learning disabilities, Marian, Hilary and Mina.

After Opening Doors Hilary wants to get a job and hopes in the end to get paid for it. She also wants to go back to college. Mina wants to work with people who use wheelchairs and Marian wants to get a job.

All of the women said that they will miss meeting each other and felt sad at the end of the Opening Doors course.

Chapter 9

Opening Doors

Mina Turfkruyer, Hilary Cooke, Marian Bridges and Jeannette Karger, with Deanne Bell

Deanne writes: Opening Doors was a programme set up to help women get into work or get back to work. It was run by Cooperative Solutions on behalf of the Essex Cooperative Development Agency, funded by money from the European Social Fund and was supported by Essex and Hertfordshire County Councils. The idea for Opening Doors came from the commitment of Harlow and Broxbourne Women's Aid to increase their services to women with learning disabilities. The programme offered teaching, training and work-experience for the women, to enable them to gain the knowledge and skills needed to support women with learning disabilities experiencing abuse. The programme also put emphasis on the women creating their own job opportunities through learning how to manage their own organisation as a cooperative.

There were nine women on the programme. Six of the women had not been working for at least a year because they were looking after someone or caring for their children. They did not have learning disabilities. The other three women also wanted to work and did have learning disabilities. These women were Hilary, Mina and Marian. These are their thoughts and feelings about the Opening Doors programme, put together with help from Deanne (one of the Programme Managers).

Hearing about Opening Doors, applying and getting a place

Mina

Jennie told us about Opening Doors. She came to Bishop's House and talked about it. There was a tape to help us, a form, and a meeting where we talked about Opening Doors. The tape said more things, it told me how to fill in the form. My mum helped me to fill in the form and she came with me to Harlow for the interview. One of the interviewers was Jeanette. She is a women with learning disabilities. She was there to interview us and she got paid.

Hilary

The interview was nerve-racking, frightening and scary. After it I felt relieved, I thought thank goodness – but I thought I'd done well. When I heard I'd got it I was over the moon. I was a bit worried, a bit nervous at times. I wanted to do something like this all along but I never got the chance to do it, people keep putting me down, saying I can't do it but I can – which I've proved.

Marian

Questions here, there and everywhere. One of the questions I asked was how I would get from A to B. It was good to see someone like Jeanette at the interview – I felt relaxed to see someone there who was part of me. I was jumping for joy – I was kissing everyone when I got the call.

Jeanette

I interviewed people for Opening Doors ... asked questions about abuse and cooperation. The questions came from us the interviewers, we prepared it, I said what I thought. I had a photocopy of the questions and we read them from the paper, there were eight questions ... some of the people had learning disabilities, some people not – able-bodied. When we actually got going it was very interesting. We introduced each other, offered them drinks, asked them where they came from and what they were doing. They were really great remarkable people! I would do it again – I was a bit nervous – but when more people came I was all right, I just got on with it. I enjoyed it once I got going ... I also got paid.

I think it's a good thing that people with learning disabilities have the same right to interview as everyone else.

Getting started and getting into a routine

Mina

There were nine women on Opening Doors some of them had not got learning disabilities and some of them did. The women that did were Marian, Hilary and Mina.

Each week we got our programme. We went to work on Tuesdays – at places where there were people with learning disabilities and at places where people stay if they have been abused – refuges. Wednesdays we had some people come into the classroom to talk to us. They did stuff like First Aid, we watched videos, we did Signing and learnt about learning disability people. Some of the teachers had learning disabilities too.

Thursdays we went to Cambridge College and we did lessons. We learnt about people dying and what it is like being upset and losing things like friends and homes. I felt it was strange when I first got there but when I met the people who were teaching us my feet came back to the ground and I felt OK.

We also did homework.

Hilary

When I went to work placement for the first time I came home and went to sleep – I was so tired, see I'd never done something like that before. Yesterday it was a nightmare, people kept coming in, people who lived there asking to use the phone. If a lady came in once she came in five times to use the phone. Well in the end I said you can't use the phone at the moment because we're busy. I didn't like saying that to her, I apologised afterwards, which I shouldn't have done really. The other staff member said, 'No, you were right really.' It feels funny being staff, you're the teacher to them instead of round the other way, them being teacher to you. It feels funny but good.

Opening Doors to new experiences

As well as the weekly routine of work-experience, training, college and home-study, the programme opened doors for the women to new places, people and experiences. They suddenly found themselves invited to Annual General Meetings, parties and conferences. The women were asked to give presentations for Women's Aid and other organisations, to talk about the Opening Doors programme.

Mina
We went on stage and talked about what we were doing. We went to the Playhouse in Harlow to talk to women who work in refuges and to day centres. We also went to London, to parties and meetings with Powerhouse [a women's self-advocacy group]. I felt nervous when I spoke but I enjoyed the people being there to listen to me.

Hilary
We went to Pyenest Day Centre and then we went to The Playhouse theatre at Harlow – I was very nervous. We went to Hackney (day centre) for a visit and Brixton – we gave a talk to people about Opening Doors ... it was nerve-racking.

Marian
We went to a party with Powerhouse and to their A.G.M. It was a good experience. Not something I'd done before.

The students' achievements

The students were accredited for attending their college modules with the chance of gaining formal credits by producing an assignment reflecting the work they had done. Most of the women chose to do this. The standards of the assignments impressed the tutors and reflected the women's hard work and the tutors' success in ensuring that their teaching was truly accessible to both the women with learning disabilities and to those without.

Mina
To help us to get a job we got a certificate. To get the certificate we had to do work at home and take it into Cambridge. It was looked at and they let us know if we'd passed or not.

We also got a certificate at the end of Opening Doors from an important man (the current Member of Parliament for Harlow, Bill Rammell). Everybody was there from work-experience, Cambridge and people from the newspaper. We all had a photograph taken and it was in the paper.

Marian

I felt really proud that I'd got something.

Mina

The women feel they have got a lot from being on the Opening Doors course, like confidence and learning to go back to work.

Hilary

For one thing I've got more confidence – I've achieved more, very much so, like going to university.

Marian

I've learnt a lot. Like learning to go back to work.

Learning together

Mina

Opening Doors was for people with learning disabilities and people without learning disabilities, which was a good thing. We enjoyed being together. We made friends. The women without learning disabilities learnt a lot about people being disabled. They learnt a lot from the women with learning disabilities, Marian, Hilary and Mina.

Hilary

It's been very good, I've enjoyed it and I mean that and all. It has been different for me because I didn't used to mix with people who haven't got learning disabilities. I've always been to college with people with learning disabilities not without and I find that very good, very helpful.

Marian

I have learnt things from the other women and have made friends.

The nine women became very close during the nine months. They developed friendships and supported each other through some difficult topics and through some difficult times in their lives. They also had a lot of fun!

Patricia

I remember Hilary nearly falling asleep a couple of times during the training sessions ... And Yvonne wanted to but Mina said 'Wake up!' and brought everyone to attention! We learnt a lot [from learning alongside Marian, Mina and Hilary]; of course we've had first hand experience as to how Marian can't get around easily. When going into cafeterias she had great difficulty with the doors and getting around the tables. It enlightened us all to what really goes on in this world of learning disability.

Ruby
The teachers gave more explanations than they would have done normally, which helped us as well as them.

Patricia
When the teacher would ask you [Mina] if you understood something and you said 'No' she'd go through it again in a slightly different language and I get it as well.

Learning about work

Hilary
I feel all right now – confident – I didn't before but I do now.

Mina
I didn't like working in the refuges. I found it upsetting. I didn't like the language, the swearing. When they cried it made me upset. I know I didn't like working in the refuges but I still felt sorry for the women who lived there. I like working with people with learning disabilities, people in wheelchairs.

Hilary
It didn't bother me. You feel for them ... but then we are not all alike, some people don't like seeing people getting upset, but it doesn't bother me.

After Opening Doors

Hilary
I don't know what I'm going to do, I may be getting a job at one of the refuges. If not I want to do voluntary work but I want to get paid later on. I am supposed to be doing the 'Equal People' Open University course as well.

Marian
I'd like to get a job, go to work.

Mina

I want to work with people who use wheelchairs.

Some of the original nine women are interested in setting up their own cooperative business to use their new-found skills helping other women with learning disabilities who are being abused. Cooperative Solutions is currently looking into funding to continue work on the development of the cooperative.

Saying goodbye

Hilary

I shall miss it very much. I will miss all my friends, I hope I will see them again.

Marian

I feel at a loss and sad, I wish it could continue.

Mina

I will miss everybody very much.

Why we wrote this chapter and why we think you should read it – Mina Turfkruyer

It is for all the people who don't know about Opening Doors because then they will know all about it.

It's for people with learning difficulties and people not with learning difficulties, which is different to like a college course. It's better, we made friends and learnt a lot from each other. I learnt a lot from them, they learnt a lot from me. I think you will enjoy reading it – the book we are making.

We were learning how to work in refuges with people with learning difficulties who had problems: arguing, breaking up from their families, their husbands, their children, moving into the refuge rather than stay at home where they have problems like being stressed, upset, kicked, hit and maybe being abused, called nasty names or sex when they don't want it.

The people should read this book because otherwise they won't know.

Then they will know, they can see. People can learn about not having abuse. Go away and think about helping the women by giving her a hand. Help by phoning up a refuge and asking if she can come in – she needs a bed, somewhere for the children to go. Think about what she wants, if she can't read or write or wash herself, sign language.

People should know that women with learning difficulties are living like this and need more help.

Easy-to-read version

Chapter 10

Rose MacDonald

by Annemarie MacDonald

It's hard to write about your own daughter. I can't be sure that I know what she thinks or feels. So what I'm writing about Rose is as honest as it can be, but may not be right. Rose might write her own story when she is older.

My daughter Rose is twelve years old and has Down's syndrome. She is very healthy. She is quite small. People often think she is younger than twelve. Rose lives with me, her father Willem, her nine year old sister Kate and two friends of ours, Ralph and Christine. We share our house, cook and eat together. We all enjoy living like this.

Rose goes to a primary school near our house. Kate goes there too. Rose seems happy at school. She particularly enjoys P.E. and learning to speak French. She is very good at remembering what she sees. She never forgets people and their names. Rose can read well. She finds maths difficult. She is quite shy with other children and likes being with adults best. But she gets on well with almost everyone. She is good fun to be with. I don't think she is bullied at school. Sometimes people think Rose can't do things that she can do. They don't give her the chance to try. Sometimes Rose is not very confident either. She worries about getting things wrong.

Rose likes listening to music on her walkman. At the moment she is keen on the Spice Girls and has pictures of them. She enjoys dancing and singing. She loves dressing up and wears some pretty wild clothes.

Rose takes very good photographs of people. She is learning to swim and ride a bike. We often go out walking. Rose can walk up to 10 miles but sometimes moans about it. She loves camping.

Next year Rose is going to high school. I hope that she will like it and that she will become more confident and independent there. I'm worried that she will be bullied in a big school with older children. But Willem and I are sure that we want Rose to be in a high school and not a 'special' school. We think that all children have the right to be in the same schools, whether they have 'learning difficulties' or not.

I find it hard to be a mother sometimes. I worry about what will happen to Rose when she leaves school. I'd like Rose to be able to live in the way she wants and where she wants to. I'd like her to have friends who think she's great.

A year later

Rose has started high school. She loves it and is doing very well. Everybody at the school has made her welcome. Rose has become more confident. She is speaking more clearly so that more people can understand what she is saying. Rose has also started to have periods. She seems pleased about the changes. It's a very exciting time for all of us.

Chapter 10

Rose MacDonald

by Annemarie MacDonald

It is an extremely difficult thing as a parent to know what your child thinks or feels. Whatever you think you know is coloured by your own feelings and experience, of love, pain, guilt that you haven't done enough. It is even more difficult when your child has learning difficulties and finds it difficult to express her thoughts and feelings in language. Rose is still mysterious to me in many ways. Everything I write here is as honest as I can make it, but it has to be read through that filter.

My daughter Rose is 12 years old and has Down's syndrome. She is very healthy except for some hearing loss, particularly when she gets colds, and short sight, which means that she wears glasses for films, theatre and reading. She is small for her age and is often taken to be considerably younger than she is.

Rose lives in a shared house with me, her father Willem, her sister Kate who is nine, Ralph, who has lived with us since before Rose was born, and another friend, who has lived with us for three years. We have always lived communally, before and after our children were born. Living in this extended 'family', which has had other short-and long-term members over the years, has been a very positive experience for all of us.

Rose has grown up with rich and close relationships with adults, in particular with Ralph. This is also true for her younger sister, Kate, and I think that this has helped the relationship between the two sisters to be strong and loving. I've read that many siblings of children with Down's syndrome feel marginalised by the greater attention afforded by the parents to the child with the disability. I don't think that this is the case with Kate, although things may change as both children grow older. In our household Willem and I are not the only adults to talk to or do things with and I think this helps avoid sibling rivalry for attention.

For Willem and I, living in this way relieves some of the pressures of living in a nuclear family – we share cooking, chores and bills, but also enjoy the conversation and company of other adults. While this kind of lifestyle can have its own strains at times, I believe that it has created a very happy and secure environment for Rose to grow up in. Willem and I are equally involved, with the support of our friends, in bringing up Rose as best we can and trying to make as many experiences open to her as possible. I find it hard to imagine how it would be to bring Rose up on my own. There have been so many decisions to make and still to make for the future. As I work part-time and close to home, most of the liaison with school and appointments with the various professionals involved with Rose have been with me.

Rose goes to our local primary school, the same school as her sister. She has been there since she was three. Before Rose was five and attending school full-time she went to playgroups at Honeylands Children's Hospital, a unique resource in Exeter for children with a wide range of disabilities. Nothing compares in our experience with the quality of professional input Rose received when she attended Honeylands. Honeylands offers well-coordinated access to physiotherapy, speech therapy, psychological and medical services, as well as playgroups and support for families.

If only services since then had been of such high quality. We have not been very satisfied with the services that have subsequently been available for Rose: they have been fragmented and patchy because of the high turnover of people and shortage of actual time getting to know Rose. Because Rose is not very outgoing socially, many people underestimate her abilities.

Rose enjoys school very much. She particularly enjoys P.E. and games, although her physical coordination means that it is hard for her to join in equally. We chose the primary school closest to our home, which had been recommended to us by other parents. Rose is the first child with Down's syndrome to attend the school.

While there have been many positive aspects to the placement, there have been some problems which have not been properly addressed by the school, or by us as parents. The school, having accepted Rose, didn't give enough thought to what inclusion really means. There has been no training for staff to help them adapt the curriculum, and very little support for the classroom assistants who have worked with Rose throughout her years at the school. The government-inspired trend away from treating each child as an individual and towards whole-class teaching, coupled with large classes and lack of resources, is an educational disaster for most children, in particular the least intellectually able, like Rose. For all sorts of reasons, many beyond the school's control or due to a lack of planning and absence of a SENCO[3] until last year, there has not been a well-coordinated or imaginative approach to Rose's learning needs. Teacher interest and input has been variable. However, she is making some progress.

Rose could read before she went to school. We taught her by using flash cards. Her visual memory is excellent. On the other hand her aural memory is poor. Her grasp of maths is very basic. Her writing is improving. She is showing an aptitude for learning French. I think our major criticism is focused on an attitude within the school that does not include Rose in a positive way.

This connects with some underlying, and often incorrect, assumptions about what she can and can't do. Her disability still seems to be what most adults in the school see. This became very apparent to us last year when a camping trip to Dartmoor was organised for her year group. A number of teachers, including the head teacher, approached us and said that it wouldn't be possible to include Rose on the trip, as there would be long walks. Rose, in fact, has more experience of camping and walking than most children. We refused to accept this and Rose had to walk eight miles as part of a preliminary exercise for the trip before she was allowed to go. Rose had to 'prove' that she could do it. And she did. But if we had been less assertive she wouldn't have gone. Outside of school she enjoys a dance class and art club.

---

3 SENCO - Special Educational Needs Coordinator.

While Rose has some friends at school, these are not close or equal relationships. However, she is a well-liked member of the school. In nine years there has not been a single incident of bullying, a considerable credit to the ethos of the school and also to Rose's sunny and cheerful disposition. She clearly enjoys being part of the school and knows the names of most of the children. One of her great social skills is an ability to remember the names of people over years. In return most of the children accept her, although she is not part of their inner circle. Many of these children have known Rose for years. It is this growing up together that is a powerful bond.

Willem and I have always believed that it is the right choice for Rose to go through mainstream education. We see the segregation of special education as wrong, both for those with disabilities and those without. Disability is just one of the many differences between people that a well-balanced society needs to accept to be worth living in. Some of the boys Rose has known since she was three at twelve are so tender with her – proof for us that integration is the way forward.

She finds it much more difficult to develop friendships with her peers and always gravitates to adults. Some of this is, I believe, due to her personality and some of it to her difficulties with language and expression. Living communally also means that we are an atypical family. We don't tend to do much with other families and there are only a few children outside of school with whom Rose has much social contact, and that of a limited kind, as her primary friendship is with Kate. Another factor is that Willem and I both work outside the home and there has, therefore, not been a great deal of 'having children back for tea'. Rose is quite shy with other children. She seems to find the noise and hurly burly of children alarming. Rose could be defined as an 'outsider' in social situations with other children. She is, of course, marked out as different because she looks different, speaks in a 'funny' way and is small for her age. However, she is a very sunny person and fun. I think everyone might describe her/himself as an outsider.

I have difficulty in determining what an 'ordinary' twelve year old might be like and, therefore, what Rose might or might not have in common. I have difficulties with ideas of what is 'normal' and in particular when it applies to people with disabilities and pressure to conform to gender or peer group stereotypes, for example. Both Willem and I were 'outsiders' because of living in other countries and our family backgrounds. This will have had an influence on Rose and also on our younger daughter, Kate, who also appears to be quite independent of peer pressure at present. Perhaps it boils down to questions of fashion and a peer group pressure to conform to it – you listen to the Spice Girls, you wear black, you play football. Is it more than this? We have never had a television and this probably also makes Rose's lifestyle different from her contemporaries in terms of access to peer culture. Rose has certainly developed a taste for black and pop music. On her own she listens to her walkman, sings, dresses up with great individual style, looks at photographs, reads simple books and funny poems. She has her own camera and takes good and very immediate photographs of people. She enjoys board games.

We find it difficult to introduce Rose to new things – she likes what she knows and often rejects what she doesn't, whether it is music or books. She enjoys swimming but is still a long way from learning to swim distances. Over the last year, she has become much more independent in practical ways and will organise herself for school and remember what she needs to do. She also helps Kate. She still doesn't initiate play with other children. One of our greatest concerns is that she tends to cut off from the outside world. It may be that listening is not very rewarding because she does not understand enough of what is being said.

Her interaction with others tends to revolve around her own preoccupations and interests, sometimes inappropriately to the situation. Often she will remember and relate events that took place a long time ago as if they had just happened. Kate, Rose's sister, compared Rose's mind to a very long train, where something that happens appears at a window long after the rest of the train has gone past. I think that this is the way that she processes her experiences, and particularly her emotions. This makes social contact difficult for those who don't know her, causes them some embarrassment and contributes to Rose's social isolation. Improving her articulation and speech as well as conversational and social skills is a priority for us.

We have told Rose that she has Down's syndrome. I'm not sure that she has any real sense of what that means. She used to deny it when we used the term but now seems to acknowledge it in relation to herself.

Rose works very much in the concrete. In retrospect, I think that we should have used the term much earlier, both with Rose and Kate. Our rationale for not doing so was because we didn't want to make too much of the name as betokening the difference. Rose had never met another child with Down's syndrome until last year. While we have always received and used literature from The Down's Syndrome Association and from The Down's Educational Trust we have never taken part in any of the social gatherings, apart from the occasional conference.

Last year I made contact with another women whom I had met before we both had children, who also has a daughter with Down's syndrome, slightly older than Rose. What was good about the meeting was that it was a way of talking to Rose and Kate about Down's syndrome and we got a book out of library to read together. Although it's not clear how Rose thinks about herself, she certainly has a sense of herself being different from other children. I think this affects her confidence in herself and in what she can do. She often says that she can't do things even when she can. Some people take this at face value. Rose is a sensitive and emotional person and picks up other people's feelings very quickly. She shows great tenderness when others are distressed and also becomes upset herself very easily when she feels that anyone is angry.

Next year Rose moves to high school. We're worried about the change and what it will mean for her. She is going to a mainstream secondary school. We looked at a couple of mainstream schools as well as special schools for both 'moderate' and 'severe' learning difficulties. Such distinctions seem very alien to our way of thinking about Rose, although both schools seemed pleasant. Practically, rather than philosophically, we have deep concerns about how Rose will manage in secondary school. Having her accepted is only the first stage in making a placement work. We have learnt some lessons from her primary school placement that we hope we can use to good effect: first, that Rose needs teacher input as well as support by a classroom assistant to differentiate the curriculum; second, that we need to be more assertive in ensuring that Rose gets what she needs from outside the school, for example speech therapy. Finally, that we urgently need to develop her independence skills and self-confidence in a more applied way – crossing the road, telling the time, getting on with things on her own. This also needs to be the school's approach.

The down side of being one of a kind in a school is that you can get away with far too much and far too little. Rose has usually had an adult at her elbow and that can create too much dependence on a surrogate 'parent'. We have had preliminary meetings with the school and are very encouraged by the positive attitude of the special needs staff whom we have met and their enthusiasm to make the placement work.

I have talked to Rose about the changes that will happen as she gets older. She is looking forward to wearing a bra. She has not yet started her periods. She knows the word 'periods' and that some of her class-mates have them, but I'm not sure that she understands exactly what will happen in practice.

The hardest thing as a parent is to think about the future. When a baby is born parents often have dewy dreams about their perfect baby, a delightful mirror of themselves, only 'better', perhaps in terms of academic or social achievement. The chip off the old block, a credit to the parents. This is nothing to do with the child and everything to do with egotism. When Rose was born, my first child, I did not have that 'perfect' baby. I had to face up to the fact that she would not be like me in many ways. And indeed, many of the things I enjoy are hard to share with Rose. But I now feel that *all* children, including Rose, should be accepted for who they are, and not who their parents want them to be. I find it a very challenging principle to put into practice. I fall short of that ideal often. My relationship with Rose is at its best when I accept her on her own terms and am not anxious about how much there is to do, about her 'progress'. What I wish for Rose is the same that I wish for Kate. That she can grow in confidence, find things that she enjoys, enjoy deep relationships with other people and be able to live her life in a way that she chooses. I would like her to be able to live independently, if she wants.

My greatest fear for her is bullying and abuse. But also that we will not allow her any freedom because of that fear. I find it hard to look that fear in the face without wanting to bury it. I know enough about the frequency of sexual abuse of women with learning disabilities to under-stand how possible it is. Looking at Rose now, she is a girl who is affectionate and physically demonstrative. She is without guile and, I think, would accept people at face value. I would never want to deny her the possibility of sexual relationships but she is vulnerable to exploitation. My dream is that she will grow up with a strong enough sense of her own worth to be able to blow the whistle on what she doesn't want to happen. I also fear dying and Willem dying. I don't trust that there will be what I call 'good services' for people with learning disabilities in the future. What will happen to Rose?

My hope is that an older Rose will read and understand what I've written here and tell me what I have misunderstood.

Postscript

Since writing, a new chapter has opened in Rose's life. She is now in her second year at Priory High School and is very happy there. Rose has made great progress in all areas. She is much more confident and her speech, in particular, has greatly improved. We have nothing but praise for the school and its staff. They have made Rose very welcome and worked hard to make her full inclusion in the school a matter of course. The school is encouraging her to be as independent as possible. She went on a trip to France in her first year, which was a great success. We have no doubt that we were right to choose a mainstream school, and this one in particular. Rose has a classroom assistant and a teacher for a day a week to help differentiate her work and liaise with subject teachers. The school is also increasingly aware that many of the teaching strategies that work for Rose can be used with other children who are having difficulties with the curriculum. We are all learning a great deal and it feels very positive. Rose has also started her periods and is managing them very well. It's an exciting time for all of us.

Chapter 11

About myself

by Rose MacDonald

We thought it was important that we heard Rose's own voice in this book. So her mum asked her some questions and this is what Rose had to say about herself.

Rose's self-portrait

My name is Rose MacDonald. I am 12. I live with my mummy, daddy, sister Kate and Ralph and Christine. I have nice hair, brown hair. I am not that small ... big! I look nice.

I like school. I like science, English, maths and French. I like the bunsen burners in science.

At home I like dressing up, playing music and music tapes. I like the Beatles, the Beach Boys and the Spice Girls. I like playing with my doll, Mary. I like reading books. Now I am reading the book *Hypnotiser*. I like the poem called 'Horrible'.

I am frightened of spiders.

When I grow up, I'm going to get periods and breasts and bras.

I have got Down's syndrome. I don't know what it is. I think I look nice.

When I grow up, I want to still live with mummy, daddy and Kate. And Ralph and Christine.

Easy-to-read version

Chapter 12

You have to be strong for the kids and strong for yourself

by Sharon Bradley and Christine Marsden with Biza Stenfert Kroese and Sarah Simpson

This chapter is about mothers with learning difficulties. When you have learning difficulties and you are a parent, you have a lot to cope with. Parents often need a bit of support, and if they don't have their families and friends to help them, there is no one else to turn to. It would be much better if parents with learning difficulties could get more support in looking after their children. At the moment, many families are split up and children are fostered out or put up for adoption.

The parents' support service in Warley tries to give the help that is wanted and needed by parents so that families can stay together and the children can grow up with their real parents. The support workers help people without judging them and are not there to sit back and criticise but to give real help whenever it is needed. Often that means that the support workers go shopping with the parents, help the children with their homework, help with decorating, or help to solve day-to-day problems with money and bills.

Here are two stories of two mums with learning difficulties.

Sharon has two children, Daniel (four years) and Cassie (three years). When Sharon was little she had to help her mum a lot because her mum was on her own and had to earn money as well as look after her five children.

As a child, Sharon was a tomboy and got into quite a few scrapes.

Now that Sharon is a mum herself, her life is very busy. She has a lot of housework, shopping, and the children demand a lot of attention. But she also gets a lot out of being a parent – the children can be good fun and now that Daniel is older she can have a real conversation with him.

When she was pregnant with Daniel, Sharon was very frightened and cried a lot. With Cassie it was a lot easier. But Cassie was born quite early and had quite a few medical problems. Sharon found it difficult to cope and Daniel sometimes got confused because his mum was away a lot.

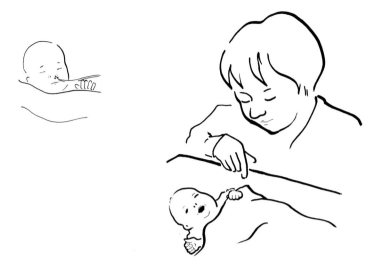

Sharon gets help from Norma, who is her support worker from the Warley parents' support scheme, and also from her mum and her sister. She regularly attends literacy classes because she is not very good at reading and writing, and would like to learn more.

Her advice to other women who want to have a child is to 'be careful and be strong because it's hard and if you're down your child is also going to feel down'.

Chris grew up with her mum and her sisters, and after she left special school she went out with a man for nine years. Nobody liked him because he treated Chris very badly and sometimes hit her.

Since then she has met a new man, John, at a disco. She has married him and they have three children together: Emma (13 years), Daniel (12 years) and Ann-Marie (8 years). All three children were born by an operation, a Caesarian, and afterwards this was quite painful for Chris. In the case of Daniel, so painful that at first she couldn't hold him when he was just born.

Chris lives near her sister, Tina, who helps her out, and her niece, Kelly, sometimes babysits. Rachel (her support worker from the Warley parents' support service) used to help Chris in lots of ways: shopping, taking the children out and sometimes just being on the other end of the phone to give advice. Rachel has now left the project and Chris has had to get used to a new support worker.

Being a parent sometimes causes problems. Anna (Ann-Marie) doesn't eat very well so Chris has had to visit the school with Rachel to discuss how to help Anna gain weight.

Daniel used to play with fire and sometimes did not get on with other children. But Chris thinks he's calming down a bit now.

Chris would say to other women who are thinking of being a mum, 'Go for it!'

Chapter 12

You have to be strong for the kids and strong for yourself

by Sharon Bradley and Christine Marsden, with Biza Stenfert Kroese and Sarah Simpson

Introduction

Biza writes: This chapter is about two mothers with young children and what it is like to be a parent, the ups and the downs.

The two women who we interviewed are being supported by the parents' support service which is run by the Warley Leisure and Enabling Services. The parents' support service started in 1995 and is supporting parents with learning disabilities in caring for their children. The part-time support workers make sure that these parents have the same rights and opportunities as people without disabilities. It gives support from pregnancy until the children are teenagers. At the moment, three support workers visit eleven families at home.

Most parents with learning difficulties have to cope with many additional problems, over and above those which most parents experience. They usually have very little money and they are more vulnerable to harassment, victimisation and abuse. They are often closely monitored by social services who assess their 'ability to parent.' This often makes the parents feel very anxious because any mistake, or any hint of not coping, may result in their children being removed. At the same time, the statutory services provide very little real support for these parents. Often resources are stretched and staff have very little knowledge and experience of people with learning difficulties. Unfortunately, there are still very few good specialist support services available to parents with learning difficulties. The Warley parents' support service is an exception.

I became involved in the Warley parents' support service because it is partly funded by the Mental Health Foundation. This organisation asked me to chair the steering group for the parents' support project, and because of this I have been meeting with the staff and the manager on a regular basis for the last two years. I have always enjoyed listening to them explaining how they work and how the families are getting on.

Last year, the steering group decided to carry out a survey to find out what the families thought of the service. I was working with Sarah, a trainee clinical psychologist, at the time and she agreed to visit the families to ask them how satisfied they were with the service. All the families were very positive and felt that it was helpful to have someone visit and support them. They gave examples: getting help with budgeting, going shopping together with the support worker, help with decorating, help with the children's homework and just having a friend who visits and who you can chat to.

The support workers also help with planning family days out and celebrating birthdays and Christmas and so on. There is a camera available to take pictures of all the special events and these are then put in a family photo album. One family was helped to plan a Valentine's Day wedding, which turned out to be a very beautiful day.

But being a parent is not always easy. Sometimes parents find it difficult to cope, especially if their children are ill or if they are having problems at school. Sarah and I went to talk to two different mothers with young children, to ask them about what it is like to be a parent. Sarah interviewed Sharon, who has two children, Daniel (4 years) and Cassie (3 years). Sharon is a single parent. I interviewed Chris, who is married and has three children, Emma (13 years), Daniel (12 years) and Ann-Marie (8 years). We have tried to write down all the things they told us during the interview, in their own words.

Sharon's story

My own childhood

I've got three sisters and a brother. I've got my eldest sister Carol, then there's me, then there's my sister Susan and my brother – my sister and my brother are twins – then I've got my youngest sister. We've been brought up by my Mom. Mom brought all five of us up together on her own because my dad buggered off with another woman and Mom had to cope with us all up on her own. Imagine how my Mom felt. I can imagine how my Mom felt now and I've only got two, so imagine her bringing the five of us up on her own. It's really hard, it's like being at work. Kids, you've got to keep an eye on them 24 hours a day because if you don't you've had it.

I was a little terror when I was a kid, I was a tomboy. No matter what the lads did I would go and do it. My Mom has like a shed in the garden and she chucked out an old mattress and an old settee and we were jumping off the shed onto the mattress, but this one – me ... instead of jumping onto the mattress I missed the settee and I missed the mattress and you know how hard the ground is, well I landed on that and it took my breath. Yes, I did that. When I was ready to leave school I got knocked down by a car. What happened was: my mate was over the other side of the road and I thought well I'm going to beat this car and get over the other side of the road to my mate. Well it didn't work, the car beat me. The point was, even my mate said it, I got back up and walked away ... I walked away from it, but the bloke stopped and took me to the hospital.

We've had our bad times as well. When I was at school there was a couple of us, one minute we were friends, then the next minute we were friends with somebody else. We were all going through that. Well this one day the girl was picking on me at school and I couldn't take it any more. I was ready to leave school and I got my own back on her, I thought I'm going to get my own back on her. I got her in the end. I hit her. I got her by the scruff of her head and I hit her.

We've gone through hell like with me Mom and that like bringing us up on her own. She had to go to work and look after us. When we was like 11, 12, we had to stop in the house and help my Mom clean up. I was always in the kitchen, did all the cooking. When I couldn't dry the washing I was going up the launderette, drying it for her. Then I'd come back and help Mom clean the house up. It's share and share alike, but Mom needed it, she needed the help. With her being at work all day somebody had to come and help her clean up and do the cooking for when she came back from work. We all had to get into it and do it, doesn't matter what happened we had to do it. What I went through when I was a kid I wouldn't put these (Daniel and Cassie) through it. I don't mind them helping me now and then but I wouldn't put these through what I went through, cleaning up and everything. I would rather do it myself.

The job of being a mum

A normal day for me is I get up in the morning, I give these their breakfasts, get them dressed, clean up. Then once I've cleaned up like, I get Cassie ready and get her to the school, then wait for the taxi to come to pick her up. Daniel gets up with us, I get Daniel dressed and while he's at school I tidy up. Usually of a Monday I go down to the school because I'm not very good at reading and writing. So I go down the school and have my reading and writing lessons. I go up the town and get a bit of shopping and it's like that every day, every day. Same thing over and over again. Sometimes it's all right and sometimes it just gets on your nerves. In five minutes when your back is turned it's dirty again and it needs doing again. The only time I shall have a nice home is when they are a bit older because at this age you can't keep it clean because it's so hard. On Sunday it's get the dinner, clean up and then you've got the ironing and then the windows to do, but you still have to keep an eye on the kids at the same time.

It's never-ending, it's like being at work 24 hours a day. Work is never finished because you always seem to find something else to do. I mean like Saturday, cleaned up, got their dinner, did my ironing, stopped in, cleaned up and in the end I did my fridge out, so you always seem to find something to do. Plus you always have to keep an eye on the kids – especially when they are babies like this – if you don't keep an eye on them they will go upstairs, go in the bathroom, turn the taps on, put the plug in, get whatever they can and put it in the sink and then you've got a flood in the bathroom. You have to be as quick as them.

You've got to be everywhere, you've got to be with them wherever they go. It doesn't matter where you go, you've got to take them with you. If you go up the town you've got to take them with you, and if they're 'on the want' they don't stop if you say yes or no. If you say no you make them cry. They're not satisfied if you do go out and buy it them because they want more. But the hardest thing is looking after them. I think it is anyway. And you've got to keep up with them. All right, at their age you can just go out and buy clothes what they want at their age, but as they're getting older you've got to get them what they want. Like they'll come from school and they'll say, 'Mom can I have' and 'My friend at school has had so and so.' So you've got to go out and get it for them because if you don't and you turn round and say no, it upsets them more.

I went out the other day because my nephew Shane has started wearing Adidas tracksuit bottoms and my son, Daniel, he only saw Shane in his and I had to go and buy him some because his face, well he was a bit jealous like – so I had to go out and buy him some.

Tuesday, I went out – they're terrible for Teletubbies here, and they've brought the glasses out now and we saw these and Daniel said 'Look, Mom, Teletubbies', and do you know, I had to buy two. You can't buy one without the other. Two pounds odd a glass and they are only plastic, and I had to go out and buy two of them. If I buy for him I have to buy for her, and it's hard because you can't turn round and say no to them and you think God, what are you doing? It hurts to say no. I don't like saying no to them but sometimes you have to say no, because when you haven't got the money it's really hard. It hurts you because it upsets them.

My mate phoned up one day and said, 'Do you want a dog?' – because it was stuck in their place 24 hours a day. They was going out, going to work, taking her son to school, her husband was at work and not one of them was going back until about eight o' clock at night. From eight in the morning until eight at night, the dog was stuck in the house and she asked me to have it. The children love it. It's calmed Cassie down since I've had the dog, plus she's been going to school which has calmed her down even more. It's being with other children, it's helping her.

The good things
The best thing about being a parent is that you have a lot of fun out of children, you can have a laugh out of them, especially Daniel. He will talk and talk to you and sing, and you can have a laugh out of him. You know you can play with them at this age but when they are really small all they are doing is sleeping, but at this age you can play with them you know, and tickle them and have a good conversation with them.

Cassie's started coming out singing now, and Daniel sings to you. You can really have a good conversation with Daniel. We went to my Mom's yesterday in that cold weather and that rain and he took his bike with him and he kept stopping. So I said to him, 'What do you keeping stopping for Daniel?' and he said, 'Well, I've broke down haven't I.' So I thought, fair enough. We got half way and then he said, 'Mom, I'm tired,' so I said, 'Get off it then and we'll push it.' It nearly killed me because I'd got her in the pushchair. Daniel holding on to one side and the bike on the other side and it absolutely killed me, it did, honest. In a way it made him happy because when we got down my Mom's, he'd got his cousins down there to play with and he was all right.

Having a baby – pregnancy and birth
With your first one you're frightened because you don't know what's going to happen. The only thing I don't like about being pregnant is you don't know what's happening inside your stomach – I mean you don't know what's happening inside. All I did when I was pregnant with Daniel was cry.

I had a lot of support with Daniel, I did. But I knew what I was going through with Cassie so it was a bit easier. With Daniel I didn't. I didn't know I was pregnant with him, but my Mom and my sisters kept saying I was pregnant and I kept saying, 'No, I am not.' When I found out I was pregnant with Daniel I was five months, then after that I was busy rushing around and getting things for him. He should have come the 1st February but he didn't come until the 10th.

I had a place of my own but they didn't want me to stop there because with your first you just don't know what's going to happen. My Mom was at work, everybody was out and I cleaned up for Mom and then about twenty to five Mom came walking in from work and said, 'What's the matter?' I told her I couldn't stand this pain no longer and she phoned the hospital for me. Took me to the hospital and they checked me over. They told me they were going to keep me in and took me down to the maternity ward but all I was doing was walking up and down the ward. At twelve o' clock they took me down and at twenty to four I'd got him – 6lbs 2oz.

I shouldn't have had Cassie, I shouldn't have had her. She was two weeks early and when she was born we went up into the ward and I couldn't really realise what was happening to her you know, when she was born. She was 6lbs 5oz, born at seven o' clock. My waters broke on the Sunday morning at five o' clock and at seven o' clock I'd got her.

Coping with a sick child

When they're bad you panic. When Cassie had that bad week, all she'd done was get on the settee, sleep, get up and get a drink and get back down and go to sleep. I thought there's something wrong here. About eleven o' clock I said, 'I can't cope no more with this,' and I got on the phone and phoned for the doctor and the doctor came out about two o' clock in the morning. Then I had to get up and phone the school at ten past eight to tell her she wasn't coming in.

When they're bad it worries you even more. They don't know what to do with themselves and they can't tell you when they're this young. Daniel can but Cassie can't and it's hard because you have to find out for yourself. I tried to put her in the bath to cool her down, wiped her with a face flannel and then I had to have the doctors and then there's another thing when they end up going in hospital. It is hard, it really is.

When Cassie was born we was in the ward and they said who's going to feed the baby. My sister fed her but she wasn't taking it and we tried to force her, but there was something wrong because she was never waking up. When they let us out of the Tuesday, we went home and she never woke up in the night, she didn't even cry. All the time I'd got her she never cried and I thought there's something wrong here. Well I didn't think nothing of it, but when I got up on the Wednesday morning, looked in her cot and there was sick all over the place, really dark green sick. The midwife came in and took one look at her and back in the hospital she went. They messed us about because we went to the outpatients first and they didn't know anything about it, so they took us to the maternity wards and they didn't know nothing about it. So we waited and they took us into the dining-room and we waited and then they took us down to the children's ward. They asked me what was the matter with her. Well, I said, she'd been sick and I don't think she's been cleared out. They cleaned her out and they said how much is she taking of her bottles. I said only drops and after that she went off them so they had to put a tube up her nose to feed her so they could get her back on her bottles. She was in three weeks and the doctor came round and said 'Did you know yellow jaundice can cause brain damage?' I said no, and he told me that it can. If it's travelling up from the feet it can cause brain damage, if it's travelling down, no. Then he said keep her underneath the window and then you'll have to go and have her head examined. Then she had to have her head examined and he said, 'That's okay.' They got her right.

Daniel didn't know what was going on. Then we got back home and we was home for about two weeks and then the midwife, Debbie, came in and weighed her and said, 'Cassie's losing weight.' I went down my Mom's the next day and all of a sudden all she did was spew up. We had to have the doctor out to her and then an ambulance and she was rushed back in again.

I was really, really down. I didn't know what I was doing for the best. Okay I've got my family but they wasn't there 24 hours a day. I was pulling myself apart, I was really ... it's a wonder I didn't crack up at the time. Her dad came up once, when she was in the hospital a second time. They wanted to take some blood tests to see why Cassie was the way she was. Her dad fled, didn't want to know. I told the sister I thought the reason Cassie was ill was that the milk was too rich for her. The sister said, 'Do you really think so?' and I said, 'Yes.' So they tried her on this Neutraprem for premature babies and she was great. Brought her home on the Cow and Gate Neutraprem for premature babies and then in the October I got this house.

With Cassie, I looked at Daniel and then looked at Cassie after, and the things that Daniel was doing, Cassie wasn't doing. I mean, at about three, four months old they are supposed to be holding the bottles, but she wasn't doing that. At six months old they are supposed to be sitting up and she wasn't doing that. They tried to give her the hearing test but she wasn't responding to it so we had to go to the doctor and tell him that she wasn't sitting up or anything. That was when they transferred me to the Development Centre and we've been going there for nearly two years and if it wasn't for them and Norma (my support worker) she wouldn't be doing the things she's doing now. She's gone through hell.

She was eleven months old when she was rushed in again for a virus. She was in for two weeks. We've gone through a lot haven't we, yes. She had to have a mask over her. You couldn't do anything with her because she was getting worse, she wasn't getting better. In the end she had to have this thing over her, the steam over her to see if she had a chest infection or anything.

This time I stopped at home with Daniel and just went up the hospital to see her. It's a nightmare isn't it, but now hopefully, touch wood, she hasn't been back in since.

We also had to go over Dudley Road, they had to put her to sleep to look into her ears. They said she's got like a whispering in one ear but there's nothing they can do really. It is really hard looking after kids, especially when they are continually going in and out of hospital.

The first time Cassie went in, Daniel was confused because he didn't know what was happening because he wasn't very old – he was only a baby himself, he was only sixteen months old. Imagine how he must have felt. I bet he was thinking, 'Well one minute my mum was here and now she's gone again, why?' You know it was hard for Daniel because he didn't understand what was going on. I came back out with her, she was home for two weeks and she was rushed in again. Then he was left behind again and he didn't know what was going on and it was hard on him again. I thought if she goes in again, there's no way I'm leaving Daniel because while she's away, I know how she's looked after and I thought, 'Well this time I'm stopping at home with Daniel.' I was taking him up there with me like, but it was hard on him because he didn't understand. One minute he was with my Mom and the next he was with his Aunty and it was really upsetting for him. Being on your own is really hard especially when you have them keep going in and out of hospital and you don't know which way to turn. It's terrible, it really is. The only support I had was from my family. This one day, my Mom came up and I just broke down. The nurse came in and turned round and said, 'Take her home. See how she feels later, we'll look after Cassie.' So I went home for the one night but I was still worried about her, and I still got up in the night and phoned the hospital to see how she was. I mean I wasn't sleeping and then I went straight up the next day. In a way I am glad it's over, I couldn't go through it again. Like I said, if it happened again I wouldn't know what to do.

Advice to other women
If anyone had to go through the same thing I would tell her to be careful ... be careful. Be strong because it's hard. You have to be strong for the kids and strong for yourself because if you're down, the baby is going to be down. This is what advice I would give to other people.

That's a picture of Cassie up there, she was really tiny, there was nothing to her. She'd just come out of hospital there but she's still poorly on that.

169

Chris's story

My own childhood

When I was little we lived with my mum and my sisters. I went to a handicapped school which was all right. Sometimes I learnt things like sewing and packing things. When I left school I just stayed at home. I wanted to go out and to have friends. I wanted to leave home, I wanted my own life, I wanted my own kids and I wanted my own flat. Then I was going out with this chap, like, nobody liked him. I went out with him for nine years. He was horrible. He was knocking me about, he was knocking me about terrible. I have a better life now, I've been married, I've got my kids.

Having babies

I met my husband at a disco and we've been married for twelve years now. We started going out together and then we got married after Emma was born. We had Emma first, she was a good baby, she was. She was brilliant, no trouble, she didn't wake up on the one bottle. If I could have another baby like her, I would, she was great.

The first time I was pregnant I went to my doctor ... no I didn't, I went to the chemist to test my water and they told me I was three months pregnant. It was a shock. My own doctor told me I couldn't have none.

Emma was a very easy baby. I didn't let anyone pick her up, that's why. I wouldn't let anyone pick her out of the cot. I used to say 'No,' and John (my husband) said, 'You're not picking her up all the time, you're not spoiling her.' John was by me when I had her, he was waiting for me when the baby was born.

I had three bad Caesareans. I didn't want no more after Emma. When Daniel was a baby, John would hold Emma and then I got caught with Anna (Ann-Marie). That's it. So I was sterilized. Me and John signed it because we didn't want any more.

Daniel was sometimes good, but when I had the Caesarean it was hurting me. I had a lot of pain, I couldn't hold him, so I pressed the bell and they took him to the nursery. I was in pain with Daniel. With Anna I only had a bit of pain but with Daniel I was having terrible pains.

Daniel wasn't naughty, but when he came out of the hospital he wanted his bottle all the time. Anna was the same like Daniel, wanted bottles and bottles. Emma didn't.

When Daniel was born my family were coming up the hospital. They were picking him up, putting him back. I thought – that's it, when they come again I didn't let them pick him up. I asked the nurses to take him into the nursery and I asked them that when the people come my husband could pick him up. I didn't want people coming in and passing him to me, I couldn't hold him. Right, I'm telling the truth, I couldn't hold him for the pains. I was full of pain, and the stitches were killing in my stomach, and my family were sitting on the bed and I thought, that's it. I want you out of the ward.

When Anna was born they had to put a tube up her nose to feed her. They didn't feed her out of a bottle, they fed her out of the tube for four days. She wouldn't breathe out of her nose and she couldn't drink properly. I nearly lost Anna, I really mean it. I nearly lost my baby.

My routine
My daily routine is I get up and get dressed and then have something to eat. Some mornings aren't too bad. Anna can sometimes get up herself; this morning she did. Emma is okay and Daniel's all right as well at getting up. Then I tidy up. I go shopping on Thursdays with Rachel (my Support Worker). Rachel takes me shopping on Thursdays. There's me, Kelly (my niece) and Rachel and Tina (my sister).

John does all the money and budgeting. He does all that, he pays all my bills. What I like best about having kids is taking them out. Brilliant. It's all right. Oh, we went to Blackpool, we did. We went to Blackpool with the kids. We didn't have any rain at all. We had some when we came back but we didn't have any there at all. We went on one of them cars, one of them things up the top and then we walked back down. It was all right. We went round the fair, we went to play Bingo. Me, Tina and Alice (Tina's baby).

People who help
Kelly (my niece) helps me a lot. When I want to go out she baby-sits sometimes. When we went to that party from John's work, she had the babies.

I go down my mum's sometimes when I've finished all my housework. We go shopping Tuesdays sometimes.

Rachel helps me a lot. She comes in tomorrow and Thursdays. She did come in on Wednesday night, I think, and went to the pictures with Emma. She helps me a lot. She helps Anna to read, and Daniel. I like them to work at school and to get an education.

I've known Rachel for two years. She's brilliant, I like her, I don't want her to leave [Rachel was leaving the project shortly after this interview took place], she helped the kids, took the kids out. Anna likes Rachel, she doesn't want Rachel to leave. There won't be another like Rachel. I miss her, I will. I shall miss her on a Friday, I will. I'll have nobody to phone. We're going to take her out for a meal, we're going to get some money and see if we can get her out on Friday. She leaves a week on Friday. It will be a big change for me. I don't why she's leaving, but she's going to talk to me about that tomorrow. I'm sorry that she's leaving. She wants to take some photographs of the kids, she doesn't want to leave. She will break down on Friday. I know she will. I shall feel terrible, I shall cry, I know I shall. Rachel is brilliant, like I said, I shall miss her. I want that in the book so that Rachel can see.

Coping with problems
The biggest problem is Anna not eating her dinners. She eats her lunch at school and then she doesn't eat her dinners at home. So that's what they are going to do, stopping her eat so much lunch in the daytime so she can eat her dinners. I've told the school to keep the lunch off her. Me and Rachel went to the school. She is putting on some weight, but she could be putting on more than that, the school said. When Anna was a baby she was terrible, when she had that tube in her. She wouldn't feed at all.

The problem with Daniel was that he was playing with fire. He had hearing problems. Rachel talked to me about that. We talked to him and he didn't want to know. So I said, 'Daniel, you're going to have to stop playing with fire.' He didn't want to know. I said, 'Daniel, you will know.' Daniel played with fire in my mum's house. My mum hadn't got a back door like us, we could get out the back door but my mum can't. She doesn't want fire in her house. He was burning everything down there, knickers, bra. When Daniel stopped down my mum's house the one night, she had to phone me back, it was terrible.

Other children were hitting him and I said, 'Daniel, you should hit them back.' My sister told him, Kelly told him, just hit them back. They did take his bike from the fish shop and they were taking all of his stuff. He's got it back now. I got it back when I went by the fish shop and I went over to his mum and said, 'That's it. You'd better tell your son to leave the bike alone.' She didn't want to know. She said that her son didn't take Daniel's bike, but people told me that he did. That's why Daniel plays up, people won't leave him alone. But he's calming down a bit now. Mark [Support Worker] comes to take him out. Rachel and Mark take the children out to give me a break.

Anna can't play out but Emma usually goes down her mates. Anna can't go out because of the road really. Someone knocked her down in the car some time ago and that's why I won't loose her out of the house now. She was lucky, she didn't damage anything.

Advice to other women
If I was asked about what it's like to be a mum, I'd say, 'Go for it.' If you want to have a baby, that's it. Say Emma was old enough, and say that she got caught, she might keep the baby and I'll look after it. Really, she wouldn't have an abortion, I wouldn't let her have an abortion. When she gets older, if she wants a baby, that's it, it's up to her.

Easy-to-read version

Chapter 13

Croydon lives

by Mabel Cooper, Gloria Ferris and Mary Coventry, with Dorothy Atkinson

Three women from Croydon told their stories. They are:

Mabel Cooper   Gloria Ferris   Mary Coventry

They worked with a helper, Dorothy Atkinson.

Their stories are called:

My quest to find out, by Mabel Cooper

Muriel and me, by Gloria Ferris

Then and now, by Mary Coventry

They told their stories from memory. Since then Mary has remembered some more things. Mabel and Gloria have found out some more things from records.

They have also talked some more to their families.

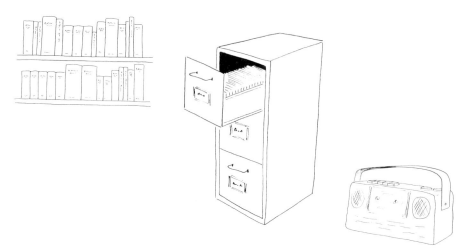

Now they are writing longer stories, which say more things.

Mabel, Gloria and Mary think that it's important for women with learning difficulties to tell their stories.

These are some of their reasons:

- it helps you understand yourself a lot more
- it's something to keep, which lasts forever
- it shows just how much you have achieved in your life.

Mabel and Gloria think it's important to look at records too. Then you find out a lot more things:

- you find out the names you were called
- you find out what happened to you when you were little
- you find out the names of the places you stayed in as a child
- you find out about your family.

Mabel used to live in children's homes. Then she lived in St Lawrence's Hospital. She knew that from memory. But she didn't know why. Mabel set out to find out why. This is her story of what she did and what she found out.

Gloria's story is about living in the Fountain Hospital as a child, and in St Lawrence's as an adult. She met her friend Muriel 40 years ago in hospital and has cared for her ever since. Gloria is now Muriel's advocate, and speaks up for her.

Mary's life story is about living at home with her parents until she became an adult. She left home when her parents were getting older, and now lives in a group home. She works for People First, Croydon.

Chapter 13

Croydon lives

by Mabel Cooper, Gloria Ferris and Mary Coventry,
with Dorothy Atkinson

Introduction
Dorothy writes: This chapter contains the life stories of three women:

(1) Mabel Cooper: *My quest to find out*

(2) Gloria Ferris: *Muriel and me*

(3) Mary Coventry: *Then and Now*.

The authors all live in Croydon. They are in their fifties and they are friends. There has been much mutual support, and encouragement, between the authors in the telling of their stories. My own link with Croydon and the three authors is twofold. Years ago, in the early 1970s, I was a Mental Welfare Officer in Croydon, Surrey. I used to work with people with learning difficulties, and I had occasion to visit St Lawrence's Hospital in nearby Caterham, as well as some of the day services mentioned later in the stories, in what was then my professional capacity.

In the early 1970s, St Lawrence's Hospital housed over 2,000 people. It was a long-stay hospital, built originally in Victorian times, but subsequently extended into a huge and forbidding institution. At the same time as I drove my Triumph Herald car around the streets of Croydon and Caterham, two of the authors, Mabel and Gloria, were still living in St

Lawrence's. They had been there for years. Meanwhile, the third author, Mary, lived at home. She lived outside the hospital, but still under its shadow.

None of us has any memory of meeting then, though we might easily have done so. Instead, I met Mabel by chance years later, when she was the Chair of People First, London, and I was a Senior Lecturer with the Open University. We worked on her story together, using a tape recorder, and transcripts. I acted as her scribe, the person who wrote the story down. That first story has already been published in a book. Now we are working on another one, and the story here is the first instalment of the second story.

Later on, Mabel introduced me to Gloria, so that her friend could also tell her story. Gloria and I have worked together in the same way: taping our conversations, putting them into words on pages, and arranging them into a story. When the idea for this book began to take off, Mabel also invited Mary to join in, and tell her story. Mary used two methods to produce her life story; she wrote the first draft herself and then expanded it through talking it through with me in a tape recorded interview. We then put the two stories together to make them into one.

The stories of Mabel and Gloria are here because they each decided they had a story to tell. They had each lived for many years in the same long-stay hospital, but had never met there. They got to know each other only when, by chance, they each went to live in the hospital's half-way house (Whyteleafe House) in the 1970s, on their way back into the outside world. That was over 25 years ago, and they have remained friends ever since.

Mary's story is different in that she lived at home with her parents until she was in her forties, and then, as they grew older, she moved into a group home. Mary's story is also different in that she knows what it is; she has photographs, scrapbooks and other mementoes. She knows the dates, names, events and places of importance to her, and she knows the people who mattered to her, who played a part in shaping her life and helped determine the person she became. Mary knows who she is, and where she came from.

It was different for Mabel and Gloria. They never knew home life. They were taken into the world of institutions when aged four weeks, and three years, respectively. Much of their childhood, their teenage years and their early adulthood was 'missing'. These years had gone unrecorded and unremarked, or else, as proved to be the case, there were official records, but these were held in places not easily accessible to them. They had their memories to go on but little else when they decided, in their fifties, that they wanted to tell their stories. They had half a century to look back on, a history of changing policies and practices. They could tell their stories to me, a former MWO, only because their world, and mine, had changed in ways once unthinkable.

Mabel and Gloria have supported each other in their projects, and they have worked with me separately and together. We made tape recordings of their individual memories. We visited the record office of the Lifecare Trust together and then the London Metropolitan Archives, in search of photographs, diaries, case notes and other documents which might shed light on their past lives.

We also talked one day about why life stories matter. That was the day when I turned my tape recorder on and invited Mabel and Gloria to reflect on why they thought it was important to know about their past lives. What could they remember? What did they have to do to find out more? And what had the past got to do with the women they are today?

This is an extract from that conversation.

Dorothy: Mabel and Gloria, I wondered if we could start with why you wanted to tell your stories? Why was it important to you to tell your story?

Mabel: The story was important to me because I've been wanting to do this for a long time and I wouldn't have been able to do it, only I met you. It was very important to me to tell them about St Lawrence's and the way it was when I went there. And it's been a great joy, I've enjoyed it and, for me, it's something that, you know, I would do again.

Gloria: When I went to lunch with Anne Evans, my Placement Officer, I said to Anne that I was thinking of doing a book, and she said, 'Well, why don't you?' And even Carol Hall, she's my Placement Officer now, she said more or less the same thing. It's not that easy. It's hard to know what you want to say. I asked Mabel.

Mabel: She did. Gloria said to me, 'I'd like to do it,' and she said, 'I don't know if anybody would help me.'

Gloria: I wasn't sure. I wasn't sure at the time.

Mabel: So I said, 'I'll ask Dorothy if she'll help you.' But it is difficult.

Gloria: I know but I managed to get a lot out of it.

Dorothy: What do your stories mean? What do they tell you about yourselves, your past, who you are – and what your lives were like?

Mabel: I think, coming out of St Lawrence's, and then doing the things that I do, and to find out I've got family around, and I go places. My wish is, I'd love to go to America and go to Disneyland. I would love that. Only because it would give me joy after all those years of being shut away and not being able to do the things what other people take for granted.

Gloria: What matters to me is being out of St Lawrence's, and being free, not having to go back. The staff didn't know why I went there, and they asked me why I went there, because they didn't have a clue. I would have liked to have gone to a normal school, to learn more. I could go to classes now but I do different things each day and, much as I'd like to go to evening classes to learn more about history, there isn't time.

Mabel: You see, for me, it did upset me for them to say I wasn't teachable.

Gloria: But you are!

Mabel: But I think if someone goes around and says something like that, are you going to learn? You're not! And for them to say, you know, I needed to be looked after, trained for life, I don't know how they could say that.

Gloria:	You've learnt a lot though, haven't you?
Mabel:	Yes, but who makes those assumptions?
Dorothy:	Can you say a bit about how it's done? How did you tell your stories? Were there any difficulties?
Mabel:	Some of it, like the names they called you in them days, that hurt a little bit, but otherwise I think it was great. It was something I needed to find out.
Gloria:	I think that it's nice to know about things that you've never really done and never really thought of. In another way, it brings back memories.
Mabel:	Some of it is upsetting but I think, for me, it's been great now that I know most of it.
Gloria:	I went to St Lawrence's with Mabel but they hadn't got my notes. We went to the archives, and I found something about Palingswick House [residential special school]. I wrote the name Wilde on a piece of paper, she was the dance teacher years ago when I was there.
Mabel:	I think you understand what's going on if nothing else. It helps you in understanding yourself a lot more. And after being in a hospital for twenty-odd years I think, you know, it makes you a lot stronger when you come out. It has me anyway, it's made me a lot stronger.
Gloria:	If you don't look after yourself then nobody else does.
Dorothy:	What have you got out of telling your stories? What has it meant to you?
Mabel:	I think it's been great, from the word go, and knowing. I'd rather know than not know. I think if you don't know, then it isn't fair, it's not the same as knowing. So, for me, I'd rather know.

Gloria: It makes you wonder what you've done in your life now that you're older.

Mabel: It's because of all the things that you do now that you didn't have the chance to do when you were younger. It gives you that and, OK, you've got it, you've got it for life, and it tells you everything.

Gloria: You do more now when you're older than you did when you were younger. The clothes we had to wear! You'd be wearing any old dress that belonged to someone else.

Mabel: I think it's great for me, and for Gloria, and I'm hoping that Mary's going to enjoy it. It's something that you can keep permanently and for us, for me and Gloria, because it was me that got Gloria to do it, it's been great.

What about Mary? Unlike Mabel and Gloria, she had lived at home with her parents. Why was it important for Mary to tell her story?

Mary: I wanted people to know what I'd done in my life: school, work, living at home with mum and dad. It's a different story. It's about a life in the community. I'd like my dad to read it, and staff at the group home and at the day centre.

(1) Mabel Cooper: My quest to find out

I'm Mabel Cooper and I'm trying to find out about the past, my past, and what happened to me. I'm finding out the schools I went to and why I was expelled. I keep finding out the names they called people in those days, and what they called me. I'm finding out about my mum because I've never known her.

This is the second part to my life story. The first part is done, and it's written in a book: it's called 'Mabel Cooper's Life Story' (1997). I did this with Dorothy. We met at a meeting where she was trying to get some history from people telling their stories. Then we met on the train going home and I said I would like to tell my story. I started telling her a bit about St Lawrence's and she said she would come up to London and put it on tape. And she did, she came to my home in Croydon, and then she took it, and put it on paper, and brought it back to me to tell me what she'd done.

Now I want to do my story again but in a different version from the first one. Now I can say, right, this is how I've done it, but the next one is different because I know more. This story is about my quest to find out; how I went to St Lawrence's and went through their records to see how I was put in there and all the rest of it, and all the things I didn't know when we first wrote my story. I also went to the archives in London and we went to the record office in Bedford to look at a diary from a children's home which was run by nuns. Dorothy and me have done a lot of other things as well. We've made phone calls, we've got photographs, we've got bits out of newspapers and I've talked to my family. I didn't even know about my family when I was in St Lawrence's.

There's so much I didn't know that I'm finding out now. I went to St Lawrence's and I went to the archives. Some of it, like the names they called you in them days, hurt a little bit but otherwise I think it was great. It was something I needed to find out. And going to the archives, that was great again, that was somewhere I've never been, and I enjoyed it. It would be smashing if half of this could be put in another book so it would say this is what Mabel said about this.

I went with Dorothy to St Lawrence's, and Gloria came, and we went up, and we had a look. They said we could look through their records, my records, and they were very nice to us. We sat in a little room for ages, it was 12 o' clock when we stopped, and then we asked could I take some of them away, that I would like some of them. They said to me, 'The ones you want you put on one side, and the ones you don't want put on the other side'. The ones I didn't want were not about the family, and they're not about anything that would interest people outside. I put to one side everything about me and my family.

I asked for the family records because I'd always been told that I had no one, except Aunt Edie. But Aunt Edie didn't want the rest of the family to know about me at all. Aunt Edie just wanted me for Aunt Edie, and the other parts of the family, no way! And then when Aunt Edie died, we went to her flat, and I found out I had another cousin, Marjorie, and her husband, Pom. And it all came back to me that I had people, a family.

I found out about my mum from my records. I found out that her name was Mabel Lucy Cooper. I was called after her. Her surname before she married was Staines. She was labelled as 'feeble-minded' in the records. She married a man called Cooper. The papers said that her parents were of 'superior standards', whatever that means. Posh! I had a sister called Margaret who went to Barnardos, but there are no records about her. We tried to find out more, but we couldn't. Nobody seems to know. I found out from my records that my mum was begging on the streets of London with me as a one month old baby. The police took me away from my mum and put me into the Easneye Nursery. They put my mum in Darenth Park Hospital. She ran away from this place in December 1944. She has not been seen since. I have not seen my mum since that time. All this I know from the records.

I've talked to my family as well. I've talked to Marjorie. She says different things. She says my mum was not 'feeble-minded'. She went to a good school. She may have had difficulties because of living on the streets. She was thrown out of her parents' home when she met up with Cooper. He was not good enough, or so they thought.

Marjorie says it's because she was living on the streets that she got how she was. She was not born like that. She could do everything. Her father wouldn't allow her back in because she married Cooper, and then mum went off with somebody else so, in them times, it was a disgrace and, of course, specially to my family because they were all so strict and well-to-do.

These are two different stories! But I've enjoyed finding out. I've enjoyed it, it's just that mum's not here to tell her bit of it. A lot of things have happened in my life but I'm who I am. I'll always be what I am, always! I will never change from what I am. You have to be hard. I've been in care since I was four weeks old so, for me, being in care doesn't bother me. I think you have to be a lot harder in the hospital where some of the staff were tough. I had no trouble with them because of Eva, (one of the nurses) but I think, if I hadn't, they could make life very difficult for you.

These are some of the things the records said about me when I first went to St Lawrence's:

I was an 'imbecile'. This really hurts.

I was 'educationally very backward'.

I was 'ignorant of the four rules of numbers'.

I was 'dull and slow in response' and did not seem to have any general knowledge at all.

I was 'not able to learn to tell the time'.

You see, for me, it did upset me for them to say I wasn't teachable. I think if someone goes around and says something like that are you going to learn? You are not! And then they turn round and say, 'Oh, you're not teachable'. And for them to say, you know, that I need to be looked after, trained for life. I don't know who made that decision, or who makes those assumptions. Who were they to make these assumptions?

I left St Lawrence's in 1977 after 20 years. I've done lots of good things since then:

- Chair of People First.
- Vice-Chair of People First.
- Travelling to Canada, Europe, Zimbabwe.
- Speaking at conferences.
- Running workshops.
- Teaching people about speaking up.
- Talking to children in schools about bullying people with learning difficulties.
- Writing my life story.
- Visiting family and friends.
- Drinking plenty of half lagers!

They were wrong to make those assumptions. I've proved them wrong. Some people have helped me and I want them to be put into this story. There's Flo, she's my friend, we both worked at the same factory when I first came out. I stayed in touch with her. She's great. I really like Flo, she's one person who is really important to me. She's been a great help to me. I used to go and have dinner with her on a Monday night, but not now because about six years ago something happened so I can't do that.

But I do go and see her, she's a great lady to me – for me, she's like a foster mum. She's older than me but she doesn't act old! She's one of those old women who's got a young mind. She's lovely. She is helpful, she's very helpful! She's great, I like her.

I want to say about Mary, the lady I live with, because she's so good and so understanding and she does help with, like, the things that we can't do at home. This is something to appreciate her for. I went to Mary's from a big home. Since I've been there she has helped me to do the things I can't do, like matching clothes up, like using the shower, like keeping calm so my face doesn't swell, and like reading, if she has time.

And Foxley Lodge is a great centre, and I would like them to be put in just a little bit. It's a day centre for 22 people, and a home for two people with learning difficulties. They help us with things like knitting, sewing, cooking, telling us how much we weigh, reading and writing. It's quite small, and very nice.

There's Rita. I meet Rita on the bus, and I've made a friend of her. She works in Allders in Croydon. I'd just like to mention her.

Of course, St Lawrence's has gone now. I was a guest of honour at the party when it started to come down. Not long ago, me and Gloria went up to have a look at what they'd done to the old St Lawrence's. They have changed it to houses. The old nurses' home is now all offices. It's for the Lifecare Trust. We walked through the new houses with Alison, from the BBC, pointing out where the old wards used to be.

There's still more to do, more things to find out. One day I want to make it into another book, part two of my life story.

(2) Gloria Ferris: Muriel and me

My name is Gloria Ferris and I live in South Croydon. This story is partly mine, and it's partly Muriel's. I was born in East London, on 10th August 1939. I've known Muriel for over 40 years, since 1956, when we were both in St Lawrence's Hospital. Of course, she was quite young when I took her on, nine or ten, I can't remember just what age she was. Her parents have both passed on; she's got a brother but they don't keep in touch. I'm her lifeline, and she's mine, more or less, although I've got other relatives. They know that I go to see her and I look after her, I do things for her.

I've been away all my life, from home, since I was three years old. I went to this hospital in Tooting called the Fountain, which was for people with learning difficulties, which is what they thought I was. My parents said I couldn't walk or whatever. They said they wouldn't come and get me there, I wouldn't be able to come home, or they wouldn't come and see me any more. That was depressing. I used to cry when I had to go away from home at weekends. I've got used to it. I've grown out of that now.

I quite liked it there because I used to go the Broadwater School, a special school in Tooting. The teacher used to come and pick us up and bring us back on the tram. They didn't have school on the inside, they had school on the outside so I didn't miss out. I was at the Fountain from when I was three until I was 13. I was there till then, then I had to leave the hospital and go to a boarding school, which was called Palingswick House. My parents used to come and see me at weekends. My father mostly came, and my sisters. My mother did come. She used to buy me things that I could do, like scrapbooks and cards. I used to collect them; cut them out and stick them in.

Palingswick House was a special school for girls. It was quite a big house in Hammersmith. It was very good, I mean, we used to go to the pictures, learn cooking, things like that. You used to have to wear a uniform, it was grey and white. There were dormitories, and some of the girls used to try and get down, out of the window, and slide down the drain-pipe. I suppose they thought they wanted to get out. I didn't do it though. It was probably hot in the dormitory, or they must have thought it was fun. I would never tell on them. It was their problem. If they wanted to get out, they'd get out. If they got caught they got caught.

When I left school at 15, I went home for a while and stayed about two years. When the schools were open, and the kids would go to school, I used to have free school dinners. I went to the Elder Girls' Craft Centre in Hackney some of the time. My family were poor. They couldn't manage. My sisters were always bossing me about even though they were younger than me. I don't know how or why they did, but they suggested I go away, be put away somewhere. Not that I really wanted to because people stare at you when you first go into these places. I have quite often said, 'What are you staring at?'

That's when I went to County Hall. I had to go there to see the consultant. There was another chap there, he was blind, he came in at the same time. I said I wanted to go back to the Fountain, but mum said she wouldn't come and see me there – but she never came to see me anyway. I was 17, I was probably past the age of going back to The Fountain. It had to be St Lawrence's.

I went to St Lawrence's on 24th September 1956, and I left there in 1972. That's a long time! I thought St Lawrence's was boring when I first went there. I didn't like it. They had all these side wards, so that when people were naughty or whatever they were put in side wards. You had to more or less help out – wash the floors, make your own bed, things like that. I used to make my bed anyway, I would never let anyone else make it because it was horrible. The beds were quite close together in those days, it was a tight squeeze turning round from one bed to another.

When I first went to St Lawrence's, you weren't allowed to go to the shops unless you had a pass to go out. I remember those days. I really didn't like it there. I didn't like the food either, or their clothing. The food was disgusting. I'd wait for the staff to turn their back and then I'd put it in the pig bucket! Some of it was so bad I wouldn't even give it to a dog. They used to bring it on to the ward and plug it into the wall, wherever the sockets were. It got better over time but not to my standards.

I didn't like the clothes either, but you had to wear them otherwise you'd wear nothing! What matters to me now is being out of St Lawrence's and being free, not having to go back. I wouldn't have been wearing a nice skirt like this in St Lawrence's, I'd be wearing an old dress that belonged to someone else. But there were people there that I did like. Some of the staff were quite nice to me on the wards I've been on. They were all right but I didn't like the place itself. It was more like what they used to call an institution. A lot of the staff there, they didn't know why I went there. It's stupid, isn't it? It doesn't make sense. I could read and write, and tell the time, and look after myself.

I met Muriel in St Lawrence's when she was very young. She was on C1 and I met her there when I took over and helped the staff out.

Muriel's family came from Shepherd's Bush. I think her father owned a cafe or shop there. They were good parents, they never missed a week without going to see her. Twice a week they'd come, even when they retired to Brighton. They never missed. They were good people, they never complained. Her parents were very good to me. We used to go out together because they couldn't lift Muriel, they couldn't manage her. We used to have tea in the pavilion in the hospital grounds.

I helped the staff out on C1. They quite enjoyed it because it helped them out. I dressed them, put them in nightdresses, I was a good help to them. I quite enjoyed being with them, especially Muriel. She is a happy sort of person. She's got a lovely smile. When you take pictures, sometimes she's not in the mood for people taking pictures of her - and she won't smile, won't even look at you. She'll look the other way. I'd never forget her. I told her parents that if anything happened to them I would never forget her. And now I'm registered as an advocate to her, so I'm near enough the next of kin.

When I first went to St Lawrence's I went to the Admissions Ward; later I went to B3. It was what they called a 'high grade' ward. There was people going out, daily jobs and work, on different wards, or the laundry, wherever. I mostly went down to C1, which I quite enjoyed doing. C1 was for people with severe disabilities, people in wheelchairs, and with cerebral palsy and other things. I worked with the nurses.

Although I wasn't a nurse, I helped them out and I quite enjoyed it. I made beds, I was in the bathroom, and I was dressing them, doing their hair, and then sometimes putting them to bed, which I quite enjoyed. I loved it. I like being with wheelchair people, I've got a way with them. Although I talk to them, I know they can't communicate with me very much back, but they understand what you're talking about, very much so. Muriel was transferred to C1 because of being in a wheelchair.

I dealt with Muriel specially. I thought she was the person I rather enjoyed being with. I washed Muriel, dressed her, cleaned her teeth, did all those sort of things. I really did enjoy being with her, and a lot of other people who were there. Years ago when I helped out I used to watch other people doing what they do, and I'd join in with them. It's what I like doing. They always thank me for what I do, and what I've done with them.

I was in my early thirties when I left St Lawrence's. My first job was quite nice, it was Wrenpark Nursing Home, an old people's home up near

Whyteleafe House. I went to live at Whyteleafe, which was a home run by St Lawrence's, and I worked part-time. I met Mabel at Whyteleafe House. We found we had the same birthday. What a coincidence! We were meant to be friends. We were made for each other. My sister has got to know Mabel as well, I don't know if my mum would have if she'd been alive. I think she might have done, and dad too. I still went up to see Muriel while I was at Whyteleafe and working at the nursing home.

Then I saw this advert in the paper for a job at Purley Hospital. I got it, and I moved there, to live in the staff hostel, on October 30th 1972. I was at Purley 13, 14 years, and I quite liked it there. I did domestic work: washing up, cleaning and doing things like that. I still kept in touch with Muriel. I went to see her on my days off. When I'd finished work I used to go up there, and then come back.

I wanted to try and go up to St Lawrence's to work. I wanted to be near Muriel. I got a job there as a domestic, on the domestic staff. I used to work on what they called the 'low grade' wards, like E3. I worked on those wards as a domestic. I moved from the staff hostel at Purley Hospital to live at Isabel's house, and I was there for six years until I moved in with Norah. That's where I am now.

I moved from the wards at St Lawrence's to work at Elmwood, one of the houses near the hospital gates. It's a house attached to the hospital, and it had a group of eight people, four men and four women, living there. I was doing the same kind of work there. I washed up, I'd do the hoovering, and toilets, and things like that. I shaved one of the men who couldn't shave himself. I used to do the ironing for them as well, in the afternoons when they'd all gone out.

I was working there and I saw this advert in the paper for Highfield Road. It was like a transfer as a domestic from Elmwood to Highfield, as they were patients from Lifecare too. I used to work there and then in 1994 I got made redundant. That's when I became an advocate for Muriel. And that was the year she left St Lawrence's and went to Whitehill House to live. It's a home for 13 clients. It's quite a nice house and they've got a big kitchen.

I go to see Muriel two days a week, Wednesdays and Thursdays. When I first arrive her face lights up! She's really quite happy. I spend the whole day there, I leave there at quarter past eight at night. I get there about ten or half past ten. Muriel can't feed herself at all. So when I get up there I feed her, wash her, bath her, do her hair, put some cream on her face. I do everything for her! And I put her to bed. I'd like to visit Muriel more than only two days a week. It would be nice to see her every day, but it's difficult getting there.

It's what I really like doing, I like being with Muriel and people like her. It's what I am. I like to help, and I like to mix with other people. I'm part of Muriel's family now. I always thought she was special. She looks forward to it, too, and I think she must miss it when I'm not there. If you've got a tongue in your head to speak for yourself then you speak up. Like Muriel, she can't speak, so I speak for her and ask for the things that she needs done for her. That's what they call 'being an advocate'. Doing the things that she needs and what she wants. I love it. I love life as it is now.

(3) Mary Coventry: **Then and now**

I lived with my parents at Bradmore Way in Coulsdon, Surrey from when I was born until I was an adult. During this time, my parents cared for me and took me to many places. My brother, Roger, was also helping to look after me. My mother made all my dresses for me. She also taught me to speak, knit and sew, as well as encouraging me to do various things. Sometimes I was good and sometimes I was naughty. If I was good I got praised, but if I was naughty I got scolded.

My parents

My dad was born in 1904, my mum was born in 1905. They were married in 1932, on 27th February. Dad said they met when they went to Paris before they were married. He showed me a photo of mum when they were young, and they were in Paris. My dad was born in Hackney, mum was born in Birmingham, in Bowden Road, I think, because my grandparents lived in Bowden Road. I used to go there every school holidays, my brother and me, when we were children. They were in Hall Green.

They moved to Coulsdon in March 1932, when the two houses were built. They were a pair, their house and another house. They lived there all their married life; 65 years to be precise. They had their 65th wedding anniversary this February. Roger was born on June 12th 1937, he was the first of their children, and I was born on 18th February 1944. He's 60, and I'm 53. He was 60 this June, Roger was. At the home we've got photos of us when we were young.

My school days

As I grew up I went to two different schools. They were St Andrew's School in Caterham and Carew Manor School in Wallington. I started going to St Andrew's when I was five and left there when I was 12. St Andrew's was a private school. The uniform was navy and white. In those days I used to take a few biscuits and an apple to have during breaks, with a drink of milk. Then I'd go home for dinner, then go back to school in the afternoon for more lessons, then home for tea. Then at the age of eight I did homework, but not during the summer, only spring, autumn and winter.

When I left I stopped homework altogether and went to Carew Manor when I was 13. I suppose you could call this a special school. When I got to a certain age they decided to stop it. It wasn't because of anything I'd done. My teacher said I'd been a credit to the school. It was a mixed school. I had to wear a uniform there as well. I had a royal blue cardigan, and a white blouse; a royal blue and old gold striped tie, a grey skirt and socks, and black shoes.

Life at home

The thing is my mother took me away from Carew Manor because it wasn't very suitable. She took me away from there when I was 15, and from then on I stayed at home for five years. I was sometimes very naughty, screaming, and having temper tantrums – it was all that screaming business. I did it because I was in a bad temper, a bad mood. And I used to do it at home as well. I was sometimes very bad tempered. I think I did it to get attention. I think that's what it was. I also had this destructive habit of picking at my clothes; sometimes I would pick whole hems undone and pull the thread in my woollens so that they had holes in them. It made more work for my mother, not less. Sometimes I got sent up to my room, sent to bed early, or sent up there to calm down.

In my young adulthood my mum did say to me that if I didn't behave I'd go to St Lawrence's so fast my feet wouldn't touch the ground! But she only said it once. We only went there for open days, that was all, in my younger days.

Mum was a Red Cross nurse during the war, then she took nursing up again with the Red Cross. And very often on exam nights, if she was having an exam she would take me with her. People practised their bandaging on me. On Monday night, an ordinary Red Cross night, I stayed indoors, but if it was exam night she'd take me with her. People practised their bandaging, and I could do some as well. She'd do it at home too, practise on my head, all different parts of my body.

Mum used to wear a navy suit in the winter, and a blue dress in the summer, and a white Red Cross cap and apron – which I have now got! She didn't want them, and I dressed up as a Red Cross nurse when I went to Waylands Day Centre because they had a VE Day parade, and I wore two of her medals and I dressed up as a nurse. I wore a blue dress, white Red Cross cap and apron, black stockings and shoes, and I looked like a real nurse. All I wanted was a petersham belt.

Mum was a commandant. I was an associate member years ago, so was my dad. We had badges. When I was 16, mum asked if I'd like to be an associate member, helping at jumble sales. I've still got my badge.

While I was at home my mother had a letter from the council to say there was a place for me at Purley Centre. I went there every day by coach. After going to Purley Centre for one and a half years, I went to Caterham Centre for eight and a half years. Then I went to Waylands Day Centre, where I still go. In the early days, I travelled by coach to Waylands, now I travel there by bus. I have been travel trained for the journey.

Leaving home
I left home on March 24th 1986. My parents were talking to me about it. They said if they died, if anything happened to them, they would like to know that I was being looked after. They wanted to get me settled while they were still alive, and I accepted it. Mum had very bad heart trouble anyway which meant she couldn't do much and she had these very bad turns at times. She's been in hospital quite a few times, had one pacemaker put in but it didn't work. She had to go back in and have it dug out, and have another one put in. Then she's been on tablets ever since. Now she's dead.

They took me into the front room one day, we were sitting in the front room, and they said about going to Northampton Road. I said, well, that would be nice. They said there wouldn't be anyone to look after me in Bradmore Way, which is where they lived in Coulsdon. Mum said that all my weekday activities would be looked after in Northampton Road – it's a group home for people with learning difficulties.

I moved in on March 24th and I was nervous at first. Every other day it was temper tantrums and screaming, and I had to go upstairs to my room. And I was crying, I missed home. But I have accepted it. I wouldn't know how to put things right if they went wrong, like if the cooker goes wrong or the washing machine. That's why they wanted me to go in there.

My life now

My mother died on April 13th 1997, and I went to the funeral and the cremation. A lot of people say I take after her. And a funny thing, I went to visit my mum in Mayday Hospital the day before she died, and one of the staff took me in to see her. When I was in there, in the ward, a nurse said to me, 'Are you her daughter?' I said, 'Yes, I am.' She said, 'You look just like your mum'. I said, 'It's because I have glasses.'

She was 91 when she died. As a young girl she was not a very strong person because she had kidney trouble. The doctors told her mum, her parents, that she wouldn't live to adulthood. She proved them all wrong! She lived to the age of 91 in spite of being one of life's 'delicate children'. My dad will be 93 next month. He has a bit of angina and takes tablets twice a day.

It's a mixed group where I live. One of the men died and another one moved out because he had been violent, so there are only two men and five women now. One woman took the place of the man who died. Since all this has happened I've now got a bed-sitting room. I've got an arm-chair in there now, and a table, my own combined TV and video recorder. I'm going to have a kettle up there as well, and dad's going to get me one of those Anglepoise lamps.

Kathy gave me the job of secretary at People First, Croydon. Somebody else did it first, then I was given the job and I'm still doing it now. As well as office work, I also work in a charity shop and go to Waylands Day Centre, I go horse riding and ballroom dancing.

This is my story. I am who I am. I wanted to tell it so that it could be published, so that I could have a book.

Messages from Croydon lives

Who do we want to read our stories?

People with learning difficulties; people we live with, our carers, family and friends; social workers, and other social services workers; teachers and researchers; doctors, psychiatrists and psychologists; TV and newspaper reporters and politicians.

Why do we want people to read our stories?

Although St Lawrence's Hospital has closed, some hospitals are still open and others don't even plan to close down. In 1998, it was estimated that 15,000 people still lived in long-stay hospitals (Bewley 1998). Many other people with learning difficulties live in big homes in the community. This is very shocking. We thought that when somewhere as big as St Lawrence's closed down they would all close. But they haven't.

We are telling our stories so that people today learn from our experiences and do things differently, now and in the future. If they don't listen, and they don't make changes, then all those things that happened in the past might happen again in the future. And we can't have that.

What messages do we want them to take from our stories?

- We want people to know what life was like in the past. We want people like social workers and MPs to understand, to know what it was like to be put away all those years in long-stay institutions. We want all the rest of the institutions to close down.

- We want people to feel ashamed of what used to happen and what still happens, and to realise that no one can learn if they live 20 or 25 years in an institution. Probably they didn't realise what they were doing because they were frightened of us. But we were frightened too. Now there's no excuse for not knowing. It's all in our stories.

- We want people to stop using names like 'mental defective' and 'imbecile' like they did in the past. We want people to stop saying 'mental handicap' as they sometimes still do. We want people to stop calling us names and teasing us. We want people to use words sensitively and with care.

- The main message is: include people, don't exclude them. What can you learn if you are shut away from life? You need to involve people in every part of life and in all things.

Part IV

Relationships

Introduced by Dorothy Atkinson

In a sense, the whole book is about relationships. This is not surprising. The stories are told by women, and they range across the whole of human life – together they capture the richness, diversity and complexity of the lives of women with learning difficulties in the second half of the twentieth century. Women's stories – whether women with or without learning difficulties – tend to be about relationships; about the people who matter, or used to, and their relationships with them, rather than a systematic or chronological account of life events (Thompson 1988, Atkinson and Williams 1990).

The emphasis on relationships in this book, as elsewhere, is because they matter. They are of central importance to everyone but they are of particular importance to people with learning difficulties whose worlds may have been impoverished through the policies and practices of separation and segregation (King's Fund 1988). People with – and without – learning difficulties define themselves in terms of their relationships with others. Relationships also help people establish where they belong, and they help confirm and validate their experiences (Firth and Rapley 1990, Bayley 1997).

Relationships bring at least the possibility of intimacy, love and belonging. They can also bring the opposite. The stories in this book bear witness to the multi-dimensional nature of relationships. There are heartwarming accounts of love and friendship. But there are more chilling stories on the other side of relationships. The women in this book make clear that relationships are the source of pain as well as pleasure; they can bring abuse and violence, as well as support; and they can leave people feeling lost, alone and abandoned.

Although the book is *all* about relationships, the four chapters in this section take this as their central theme: 'Oma', by Mina Turfkruyer; 'Death and bereavement', by Pam Barette; 'Hoping everything works out', by Susan Ashurst; and 'My story' by Christiane de Burg. These stories, between them, convey the essence of what it is to be a women with learning difficulties – and they do so from the perspectives of a grand-daughter (Mina), a daughter (Pam), a wife (Susan) and a mother and grandmother (Christiane). These stories have some claim to universality in that they cross national boundaries, capturing Mina's experience of spending time in Holland with her Dutch grandmother, and tracing the ups and downs of Christiane's life in her Belgian homeland.

The authors of the four stories have not written glowing accounts of happy lives and loving relationships. No one lives happily ever after. Quite the contrary. They speak instead of the losses in their lives – the loss of a much loved parent or grandparent; the loss of a husband, and a marriage; the loss of hope and trust, through violence; the loss of children; and the loss of freedom.

There are many regrets, and there is much sadness. Mina still misses her grandmother; Pam still mourns not 'just' the loss of her parents, but also the loss of her home, the loss of all keepsakes and mementoes, and the missed opportunity to say goodbye. Susan is alone and lonely; she misses her husband John, and mourns the loss of her marriage. Christiane looks back on two failed marriages, and all the losses she has suffered through them – not least her early miscarriages and, later, the loss of her daughters. Along the way she also lost some of her capacity to trust people because no one listened to her, they only listened to her abusive husbands.

Relationships matter. When they are loving and supportive, they bring many gains. Thus, although Mina misses her grandmother, she looks back with pleasure at the happy times they had together. But what happens when relationships go wrong? That's when, according to the authors of these stories, people need someone to talk to: someone who listens, and who understands. This is a common theme. Pam's feelings might be different now if her cousin had listened to her when her mother died; and later, if social workers and others had listened to her about what she wanted in life and where she wanted to be. She was placed in a group home, which she hated, just as, hundreds of miles away in Belgium, Christiane was placed in a group home following all of her losses (and which she also disliked). The public and shared life of a group home is evidently no automatic substitute for the intimacy of a family or marital home — however mixed the experience of the latter might be.

Christiane is very anxious now to speak out about her life, and anxious that people should listen. She feels that women with learning difficulties need to be listened to with respect and understanding because there are many people — including the men who actively seek them out — who take advantage of them. She was just such a person and no one listened to her or, if they did, they did not believe her. As Susan's marriage foundered, and then began to come apart, her other relationships became of paramount importance to her. They kept her going. They helped her cope, and feel less alone and abandoned. She found support, both emotional and practical, through having people to talk to — and who listened to her. They included family, friends, neighbours and social workers.

These stories about relationships pull no punches. Women with learning difficulties, according to Christiane, want to be like other women and to have the opportunity, if they so choose, to get married and to have children. But these options, while carrying the potential for happiness, also carry many risks. Women with learning difficulties need positive and supportive relationships in their lives during the good times as well as the bad. They need people to talk to who will listen to them and understand what their lives are like. This is a book of women talking about themselves and their lives. It is up to the rest of us to listen and to understand.

Easy-to-read version

Chapter 14

Oma

by Mina Turfkruyer

We used to go and stay with my Grandma for the holidays. She lived in Holland. We used to go there at Christmas as well.

At Easter Oma (as we called her) used to come and stay with us.

We used to go out for rides on the bike.

Oma came with us. Or we went out for long walks. I held Oma's hand. She used to cook our meals. She came with us on visits to other members of the family. She gave me presents for my birthday. One day she became ill. She had to go to hospital. She was ill for quite a long time. We could not stay with her anymore. And she could not come to England anymore.

At first, my aunt looked after Oma in her own home. But after few years she had to go into a home because she needed a lot of looking after. Gradually her condition worsened. We went to see her in the home during the summer holidays. She was very ill by now and quite confused. A few weeks after that Oma died. My mum and dad had to go back to Holland for the funeral.

There is a nice headstone on her grave. We visit it some times. I wish she was still here. I miss Oma.

Easy-to-read version

Chapter 15

Death and bereavement

by Pam Barette with Jan Walmsley

I lived at home with mum and dad till dad died.

My dad died on 7th March 1987, in my house in the living room. The man came with the coffin. I was crying.

Dad left me and mum on our own. Mum drinking a lot. I did everything. Washed her, dressed her.

The ambulance men came in. Take her to hospital. Can't talk. I touched her fingers. I took some flowers for her.

She died in hospital not my house. When I went back she's not there. They taken her away.

I went to live in a Group Home. It was terrible cos I'd just lost my mum. I wanted to stay in my old house. It's not nice there, lot of trouble there. I do cooking for them. I don't want that. I want to do it on my own but if I don't do it I get told off by the manager.

Chapter 15

Death and bereavement

by Pam Barette with Jan Walmsley

Introduction

Jan writes: I have known Pam for a long time, and I knew she had strong feelings about her mum and dad. So it seemed a good idea to ask her to write something about that. We met in East London where she works for a voluntary organisation and I asked her to tell me about her mum and dad. This is what she said. I tape-recorded our conversation and went away and wrote it up. When I went back to her with it I read it out to make sure she agreed with it. Then I asked her what she would have liked to happen when her mum and dad died. What she said is written down as a list at the end of the chapter.

Pam would like doctors and social workers to read this so they will learn to treat people's feelings with more respect.

Dad's death

My dad died on 7th March 1987 and my mum died on 26th December 1989. I lived at home with mum and dad until dad died. He died before my mum. Dad died in my house, in the living room. He hadn't been ill before. Mum said, 'Don't come in the living room.' The man came, with the coffin. I went to the graveside and I was crying. Dad left me and mum on our own.

After dad died

I lived with my mum after dad died. That's why I left the Centre, look after my mum, she taken ill, I got sent home with her. Mum drinking a lot. When me dad died, she drinks more. My mum keep on drinking, stop her thinking of him. I did everything. Washed her. Dressed her. She couldn't feed herself and I fed her. I coped, yeah. My cousin couldn't believe her eyes, what I did for mum. I coped.

My mum took a lot of tablets, blood pressure tablets, water tablets, doctor gave me those little packets. She took 15, 16 tablets a day in her life, one white, one blue, make her go to toilet, she had everything, make her feel better. Tablets not working on her properly, make her go to toilet, too many tablets in her life, accidents she had, too many tablets, some not working on her properly.

My life, I used to pour the vodka down the sink, bottles of it, down the sink. Drinking, and I stopped her.

Mum's death
The ambulancemen came in, yes, the ambulance men. I gave them her tablets, take to hospital with her. The liver, it was, she been drinking a lot. I went to the hospital a couple of times to see my mum. She was alive. The consultant doctor said to me, 'You know what the matter is, your mum likes you too much.' I says, 'I know she does.' She was all black and blue. Can't talk. I touched her fingers, she even move her fingers a little bit. And then I took some flowers for her. And I said, 'It's me, mum.' She no answer. And my cousin said to me, 'How is she Pam?' I said, 'I don't know. I need your help on this.' Nurse took me in the consulting room and the consultant doctor came into the room. I said, 'What's the matter?' And he said something to me about my mum. He said, 'I know you love your mum, your face got your mum's look.' And he said, 'I got sad news.' I sat there, quiet. He said, 'Your mum won't live.' I sit there, bursting out crying. I said, 'What we going to do, I can't do anything my mum's not there.' She died in hospital not my house. When I saw her she was alive. When I went back, she not there. They'd taken her away.

I got a message for mum:

Dear Mum,

I find it very quiet when you are not here. I do miss not being able to ask you things. I'm going to arrange to have your name put on the gravestone.
Pam

What happened after mum's death

I got no counselling. I said we'll make something. We'll get her a grave-stone. I can help, but I don't know where it is, the big place where they make gravestones.

I never went back to the house where I lived with my mum. My cousin took the keys away from me. She told me I didn't want to go in there, give me bad memories of her. I wanted to go back, I wanted to take all the washing to the laundrette, clean the house up. It's a mess, my house. I wanted to do something, I had to do it, but my mum want me to do it, not my cousin. Mum wanted to do it for her sake, not my cousin's sake, she wouldn't do anything to help my mum. I got telling off a lot from her.

My cousin took the keys, gave it to the next door neighbour. All I want was a photo of that house, remind me of it. My cousin threw it all in the dustbin, everything what was in that house. Mum said, 'Dad said any-thing happen to your mum everything belong to Pam Barette.' Everything. It goes to me, not June, my cousin didn't get any of it. It belongs to me, in my name. I live in that house, and house belongs to me, not my cousin. She threw it all away, that's what she did.

I go to the grave, City of London Cemetery, Bridget took me, on their wedding anniversary.

A new home

I went to live in John Kirk House. It's a Group Home, in Beckton. It was terrible, cos I'd just lost my mum. I wanted to stay in my old house.

It's not nice there, lot of trouble there, with Alison's there. I can't talk to her what I feel like. I said to Alison, 'You like Robin too much. He knocked me on my arm, got a bruise on my arm. How would you feel if Robin did it to you. You'd suffer, be in pain.' She said, 'Don't talk to me like that.' I said, 'Robin makes up to you, calls you sweetie, makes a fuss all over you.' So she stops me going places, like here.

I said, 'I'll tell my cousin when she comes tomorrow, I'll tell her every-thing you done to me.' I get a lot of trouble there. I want her to do some-thing.

I don't know why, I do cooking for them. Robin don't like cooking. I don't want that. I want to do it on my own, but if I don't do it, I get told off by the manager.

I'm moving into my own house in Forest Gate in September. Do my own cooking there, on my own.

What I'd like to do:

- Write to the hospital, ask about papers about mum's death.
- Talk to my solicitor in Deptford about the will.
- Find mum and dad's birth and death certificates.
- Take a photo of my old house.

What does Pam's story say about how to help people when parents die?

Make sure people can get access to the records of their parent's death and can make copies.

Let people say goodbye to their mum or dad.

Help them find a gravestone, and decide what to write on it.

Allow people to go back to the old house and choose some things to keep.

Make a scrap book to help remember. Put in it important papers, documents, photographs, stories, poems, souvenirs.

Arrange regular visits to the grave.

Get something to keep.

Make a book.

Easy-to-read version

Chapter 16

Hoping everything works out

by Susan Ashurst with Bridget Whittell

Susan talked to Bridget Whittell, who helped her to write this chapter. Bridget taped what Susan said and then later wrote it down.

In her chapter, Susan talks about people who are important to her and about relationships. She talks about her family, her husband, her friends, her social worker, her tutors at college and her neighbours.

Susan met her husband in 1987 and they got married the following year in 1988.

Different problems have made life very difficult for Susan recently and she describes how these have been making her feel. The problems Susan has had to cope with include:

- Her husband being ill in hospital, leaving her on her own and feeling lonely.

- Having to manage and pay the bills, but forgetting to renew the TV licence.

- Coping with difficult and nosey neighbours.

These problems have made Susan worry a lot. They have also made her shout and argue with her husband. Susan's husband left her and went back to live with his mother.

Susan needs people to help her cope and get her through the difficult times she is facing. She describes how family, friends, social workers and a friendly neighbour have been helping by:

- telephoning, visiting and listening to her, giving emotional support.

- giving practical support by helping to sort out the bills and doing shopping.

- keeping Susan company when she is feeling lonely.

Life continues to be very difficult for Susan at the moment. It is very important to Susan that she has someone to talk to and people who can help her through the difficult times.

Chapter 16

Hoping everything works out

by Susan Ashurst, with Bridget Whittell

Introduction

'This chapter is about me being married and finding it very difficult at this moment in time.'

Bridget writes: I have known Susan for about eight years now and we know each other quite well. Susan belongs to a self-advocacy group that I provide support to and we also talk together quite a lot on the telephone. We have also been along to women's group meetings together, a local WILD (Women In Learning Disabilities) group. It was through the WILD network that I found out about this book and asked Susan if she would be interested in contributing to it. She said she would be and when we first met to talk about what might be included in this chapter, Susan explained that she wanted to be able to talk about how she has been feeling and finding things difficult over recent weeks and months.

So, Susan talks about her feelings and how different people have been helping, or not helping, her to cope as she has experienced problems and gone through a particularly difficult time in her married life. This chapter is also very much about relationships and some of the important people in Susan's life. Five of the conversations we had together at Susan's flat were taped, and this chapter – using Susan's own words as much as possible – was put together from these tapes. However, it has been an extremely difficult and emotional time for Susan. Many of the times we have met together have not been to talk about the book at all, but just to talk, and me to listen.

Family

I was more close to my dad than I was to my mum. My dad just recently got married again, not so long ago, I think it's about twelve months. They live down south. I went to the wedding. My new stepmum is all right, you know, I get along with her. If I want anything doing, she listens to me. I really miss my dad since he moved away. I know basically he's only on t'other side of the phone, but like over Christmas, when he went away on holiday, that's when I really needed him.

I've got one brother, Dave, a real brother. And I've got four stepsisters. One's our Sandra what lives round the corner and she's got two children, so I've got a nephew and a niece. The little lad is seven and the little girl's just turned five. And then there's our Anne and I've got a nephew and niece there. And I've got Jayne, and she's just recently had a little lad. She lives down south, near my dad. And the other one, Carol, I don't see much of her. I see quite a bit of our Sandra and Anne, and sometimes our Dave when he's not working. I can go round to our Sandra's at any time I want, because she's only round the corner. Sometimes Sandra will say, 'Will you baby-sit for me?' Sometimes I'll say, 'Yeah, if I'm not busy, I'll do it.'

Meeting and marrying John

I met John when I went on a residential weekend in 1987. There was a few of us from different training centres that went. I knew the people that went from our day centre, but not from the other ones. It was really good that, getting to know people and meeting people. I wasn't bothered about meeting anybody. John wanted me to sit on his table, with him, to have a laugh and a joke, you know like you do when you're friends. So I did do, and he wouldn't let me go to anywhere else, he just wanted me to stay there, that weekend.

After the residential I got one of my friends to write him a letter, and he wrote me one back, and somebody read it to me ... so we wrote each other letters, just friendly letters ... and then he phoned me up and said, 'Would you like for us to get to know each other? Is it all right, Susan, if I nip down?' and I said, 'Yeah'. And from then on, we started going out. He used to come to the hostel to pick me up, and we used to go out, and we just carried on like that. And he used to come down to the bungalow[4]. A couple of nights he stopped, when he couldn't get home. I eventually moved out of the bungalow and moved into a house that was privately rented.

We got married when I was 24, in 1988. When I got married I was at college – I'd left the training centre – but they was all supporting me from the college. Maureen, a friend, was at the college with me. She came to my wedding and she came to the reception at night. All the family were there. We didn't go on honeymoon ... we didn't have the money. A bit later on, my dad paid for us to go on holiday, so we went away then. It was the first holiday I'd had for a long time.

We lived at the rented house after we were married for quite some time, but the reason that we moved out was because the landlord wasn't repairing anything for us. I paid the rent every week and I kept complaining about these jobs that needed doing, like when it was raining very hard, we had to keep putting buckets and bowls down. I was paying so much rent for it, I was really raging. John said to me, 'I'm not living in here any longer, I'm going to me mum's,' so we ended up moving down there.

Living with my mother in law, it was really difficult. Before I lived with her, I got on smashing. But it was different when I went to live with her, it was different all together then. It was very difficult, because basically John had to do what his mum wanted doing. I kept saying to her, 'Look, we're married now, we should be able to do what we want. I know it's not my house or anything, but a married couple should be able to do what they please, when they want.' But in some ways she weren't that bad. I mean, we used to go out at night into a pub round that end. And we enjoyed it, apart from her being there all the time. That's one of the reasons that I eventually moved because, you know, we've got our own lives to lead, so she can't always be there all the time. We've been here in this flat roughly about two years now. When we first had this flat[5], there were nothing in here.

---

4 Independent living bungalow on the site of the residential hostel. Susan moved to the bungalow after leaving the hostel.
5 Susan and John put themselves on the housing list a few years ago and moved into their present flat about two years ago.

Coping in difficult times

Illness

John was ill over the Christmas period and had to spend a few days in hospital. Susan talked about this during our first taped session in January.

I'm going through a really bad patch at the moment with John. I phoned my sister a couple of weeks back and I said: 'I really needed somebody to talk to,' and she said: 'Why, what was the matter?' and I said: 'Well, John was away, John was in hospital.' She said: 'What was the matter with him?' I said: 'I don't know. He's just completely lost a lot of weight.' He was just wasting away ... and I just needed somebody.

Our Sandra said to me when John was in hospital: 'If you've got any problems, either give me a ring or come round,' and then she'd pay my electric, gas, water and get all my bills sorted out for me. But normally I can do that myself; it's just that when John was away, I just needed that bit of help. My sister said to me, did I want to sleep over at hers when John was in hospital. I said: 'No, it's no good me coming and sleeping over. I'm not being funny, but I'm thinking about our Diane,' because our Diane, my niece, would have given her bed up for me, and she's only five, and I didn't want her to do that, so I slept in my own bed, but it was very frightening. Even though I had my neighbour with me, and she'd got her dog who protects my house as well as she protects my neighbour's house, but ... I just needed somebody ... I needed somebody to talk to. When I'm here on my own, I don't have the telly on, I don't have the radio on, I don't have the fire on, I don't do anything ... I just sit here, on my own, and that's it.

Stress, money problems and difficult neighbours

On this next visit, Susan was very upset after a big argument with John the previous week. John had gone to his mother's and had not been back for a week. Sources of tension included money worries and problems with some of the neighbours. Susan and John had forgotten to renew their TV licence when it expired and when Susan was out one day, the television people had called on John and threatened prosecution. They had had to renew their licence, which only had a few months to run before it needed renewing again. This was an unexpected burden on their slender financial budget.

I've been on my own ever since last Thursday, and I can't, I just can't cope. It just started ... because I shout at him a lot. I don't mean for to shout at him though. I'm shouting all the time, and I don't mean it. I can't do anything about it. I know last week John went and stopped and had a couple of minutes with our Sandra. He went and told her that I got him into trouble. And I really got angry. I just can't help it ... and I had me neighbours complaining and talking about me and everything. I mean, I'm very frightened of saying anything to him ... because all me neighbours hear me and that.

That day we went to London[6], about half past two, the telly folk came ... they were just in plain clothes. I had no licence, so we couldn't watch telly and we had to go across to our neighbour and watch it. We've got a licence now, but only from my Disability Living Allowance – £95 for a colour licence. Each week now I'll have to get the stamps till June again. I thought it would have been all right till this year, but I weren't, I got caught. The neighbour upstairs, she wrote a letter to them and spoke on the telephone to them. I've got a letter back, and they said that I might not get away with it, but they might prosecute, and that's what I'm worried about. I've got the licence, that telly is in my name, but John will be for prosecution. And I think that's what's doing it all.

I just can't cope ... I went into see one of the college tutors last week and I said to her, 'I'm packing in college,' and she said why, and I had to tell her. I were really upset. I said to her: 'I'm packing in, because every time I do anything, or I go anywhere, I just can't do it, because I'm leaving him here to do all the housework and everything, and it's not fair ...' I mean, it's not fair on John ... I don't ask him to clean up, he just does it on his own.

The neighbour downstairs, that's why we keep ... how we're falling out all the time. Because he doesn't like John. He's all right with me, but he just doesn't like John, I don't know why, he just doesn't like anybody. He starts banging about, and if we move the bins, he puts his bin first. That's how awkward he can get ... especially if I'm not here, like if I'm at college. He's trying to get John going, and that's what's causing problems and I'm getting fed up of it.

---

6 The day Susan and I went to London for a book meeting in January.

I just want my life back together again ... I need somebody to talk to. The neighbour next door she's proper good, I mean, she goes shopping for me and that. She's proper good, that way. I can talk to her, but I can't tell her about my problems like I can tell people like you, you know what I mean. I can talk to Barbara[7] but I don't see her any more, and Jackie[8]. I had a word with Jackie t'other day. Jackie brought me home from college because I was upset, she saw me, and she come back home with me for a cup of tea. But my neighbour upstairs came in, and she was in all the time. She wanted to know where I'd been, you know, and all this, that and t'other.

But I'm sick of all this trouble what's going on. I'm getting the blame for it all. When we're not together John'll say, 'Oh, it's your fault again,' and whenever anything goes wrong ... it's not fair. I just want him to come back, I don't want to be in that bed on my own.

Managing while John was in hospital
John returned home the following week, but a few weeks later was taken into hospital suffering from mental stress. He stayed in hospital for about two weeks, leaving Susan on her own in the flat again. Susan talked about how she was coping.

My next door neighbour, she's been really, really good ... and talking to people and having support there. Talking to Theresa[9], she rang me t'other day, she rung Friday night, and she was very supportive. And getting on the phone and talking to my dad, and I've been across to my sister and had a chat with her and that, and I went down to my other sister's as well ... all these sorts of things. They're all here for me, you know what I mean, but it's not helped when you're in the flat on your own. I've been going to bed about 10 o' clock at night when John has not been here. It's not been so bad during the day because I've been going to the hospital all the time ... but at night time, it's been really hard. It's the worst thing for me. If it weren't for Theresa and people like that, phoning me and getting in touch with me, thinking if I'll be okay, and doing things and helping me, I wouldn't have got through. But I've got through, but it's been really difficult.

---

[7] Support worker at the college.
[8] Someone who lives close by.
[9] Parent of a young woman with learning disabilities that Susan met and became friendly with when she attended a course in 1996.

Like I say, I'm pulling through. I'm going through a bad stage at the moment. I've things that I should be doing, but I'm not doing. I should be going out. And besides that, my sister's going in hospital on Tuesday, so that's another worry. People don't understand, but they're just going to have to. I've calmed me temper down a hell of a lot. I don't know how I've done it, but I've done it, even though I'm still wound up inside. If I'm in a bad temper, if I know that I'm going to do something, if somebody says something, or if somebody's going to do something at me ... I've got to go for a walk, I've got to go out. I've got to get out of the situation. If I could have help with that shouting, I'd be a lot better. I can feel it myself, I'm not calm enough. It's just building up all the time, and building up. And when you're not well, you bite somebody's head off. They don't understand, some of them. I mean, I've been through some really bad times you know.

The social worker said to me: 'I believe you're having problems with the neighbour downstairs.' I didn't mention one of the other neighbours, but I think she gathered that I was also having problems with her at the moment. Because the first time the social workers came, when I had to get John in hospital, that night she, that neighbour, came across. She didn't bother knocking on the door, she just opened the door and came in. 'It's only me ...' she shouts upstairs. The two social workers said: 'Who's that?' to me. I said: 'Well, it's my neighbour, she comes from over there.' The social worker said: 'Does she do that all the time?' I said: 'Yeah, she doesn't bother to knock. She just opens the door and shouts.' She's been in a few times, when the social worker has been in. She just comes in. So I have to put up with that, and I also have to put up with him, the neighbour downstairs.

One problem on top of another

After a fortnight's stay in hospital, John returned home again, but problems and tensions remained. To make matters worse, a neighbour who had previously been very helpful to Susan was now adding to the problems as Susan thought she had now turned against her as well.

When John got the DLA[10], he went in there to show her, the next door neighbour, what we'd got. She said, 'Oh, it's all right for some people like you two, you've got DLA. I'm seeing if I can get it now.' Really snotty.

---

10 John successfully applied for Disability Living Allowance after coming out of hospital.

And she's never, ever, been anything like that before. At night now, she doesn't bother coming in, which I'm not bothered about, but I wish people would start leaving me alone and letting me get on with my own life. She shouted at John yesterday again, to give John my key, so that she doesn't see me. She never said, 'Oh, why don't you ask Sue to come over.' and I feel that I'm not wanted. But that's not the way to be. I mean, I don't fall out with anybody. It's just the way that she's been. I mean, I'll do anything for her, if she asks me to put her daughter's washing in the washer, I put it in for her. I don't ask for any money, for my electric, I do it as a favour, as a friend, like everybody does. But why is it always me that she's getting at? She never gets at anybody else, but why me?

The attitude of people lately is unbelievable. I mean, I've done nothing, and why should it be me that's getting in trouble for it. It's not the way that I'm doing things, it's the way that people are talking about me, instead of being upfront with me.

John knows about it, but yet again he's keeping out of it, which is very hard for me. But if I don't get his support, I'll get me dad's. My sister round the corner's got two children, so I don't go round very often and tell her my problems. She's busy. My dad didn't know I had all these problems until my sister round the corner phoned him and she said, 'Dad's going to ring you,' and he said to me: 'I didn't know you had all these problems. If I could come down, Susan, I'd come down and talk to you.' I mean, John is all right, he's got his mother on the other end of the phone, and she's close. I said to him, 'It's not fair. You're always going down to see your mum. I don't see mine.'

I just need to get away. I'm going to have a nervous breakdown, because I've picked John up. I don't know how many times I've picked him up, but I've picked him up a hell of a lot. I've supported him ... and I need the same, but I'm just not getting it.

Finding help and support from social workers, college tutors, family and friends

The social worker's not too bad, I mean, she understands. She said to me: 'If there's any problems, like with my bills and things like that.' But I've managed all my bills, I can do that. I can manage that. I think they're there to help in a practical way. I'm not really sure, because I don't know. I've not had a social worker for ages, and it's a very odd feeling to have a social worker, because I've near enough managed and done everything myself. But, I've just blown up ... I'm just bottling it all up. Instead of telling people about it ... I can't, I can't do that. I don't know why. I just feel like ... I probably want the right people to talk to. With having so much pressure and stress on me lately ... it's unbelievable.

I can talk to my dad, my dad understands. I have a brother ... me and our Dave were the closest ones as children ... but he's not been down for ages, and I've not seen him for a long time. Sometimes I ring Theresa, sometimes I ring Helen[11], but Helen has a lot of problems because Helen's not been so good. I talk to you when I can get hold of you. That's about it.

I had to pack in college because of John. I used to talk to Beth, one of the tutors, and I used to talk to Elaine, another tutor, and I used to talk to Doreen, a helper at college. With John being ill, it's stopped everything, it's just stopped everything. I don't miss college now, but I miss going out. Sometimes I'm stuck here. If John wants to go up to his mum's I clean and tidy up. He never asks me if I want to go up to his mum's. He just goes himself. I just feel that, you know, that nobody wants me.

Hoping everything works out okay

The last taped conversation took place about two months later. John had moved back to his mother's again. Susan had been on her own for the past two weeks and was finding it difficult getting the opportunity to talk to John on his own.

I just can't talk to him when his mother's there. If I go down and say to him, 'John, I want a word with you. I'm not going to shout at you, but I want a word with you,' then I'd have to take him out, either take him to L... or take him to W... and have a look round the market, or take him into the pub and have a drink and just sit down and have a chat. I mean, if I could do that, that would help. But, what I got yesterday is, 'I'm too tired. I don't want to,' which I understand. I mean, look at me, I'm tired. But at least I'm doing it. I just feel that it's important and I just feel that I want to get my marriage back, and if I could get my marriage

---

[11] Another parent of a child with learning disabilities that Susan met on a course in 1996.

back, I wouldn't be like this. But it's up to us both, you know what I mean, to make it work. Like I say, I can't do anything. All I can do is carry on talking to him. As long as I'm talking to him, and he's talking to me, and we understand one another, which I do, I understand him, because I know he's been ill, so I understand all that. That's what I'm here for, to help him get over that. But, like I say, all we can do is talk until … whenever … I can't do anything else.

I'm just hoping that the social worker's been talking to him and that she's made him understand the way that I've been feeling. The last time I spoke to her, I was in Netto[12], some time last week, but I was too upset. She just come down on me saying, 'Hello, it's me. What's your problem?' But I couldn't really tell her, where there was a shop full of people. So, how could I tell her how I felt about John? I've not had a proper chance to talk to her. Well, I have spoken to her, but I spoke to her with a shop full of people. But that's no good, a shop full of people, they probably heard everything, and that's not the way. She just said to me, 'Do you want John to come back?' and I said, 'Yeah, I need him, because I need him to help me with everything else. I can't reckon up my bills.' She said, 'Well, do you want help with that?' and I kept saying, 'No I don't want help. I can manage it myself if John comes back.' But after that, you know, I just started crying.

I'm finding it really difficult, really hard. It has been very difficult over the last few weeks and I'm just hoping everything works out okay and that my marriage gets back together. My sister's been very supportive … the social workers have been very supportive and friends and people that know me best, but my neighbours haven't, and I'm going through some very difficult times at the moment.

Postscript

Susan continues to cope despite all the problems that she still faces. John is still living with his mother. Since they have separated, Susan has been given her own social worker. At the moment, Susan is thinking about moving out of the flat because she finds it difficult living on her own and problems continue with the neighbours. She thinks she might move away from the neighbourhood she is living in now and of sharing a flat or house with somebody else, although she realises that if she does

---

[12] A local supermarket store.

that, she would not live so close to her stepsister, Sandra. Susan finds it especially difficult not having her dad living close by and feels reluctant sometimes to get in touch with family and friends because she is sensitive to their own busy lives and problems.

It was not easy for Susan to tell this story, but she wanted to do it and wanted other people to know about the problems she has been facing. More importantly, she wanted to be able to tell her side of the story and for people to understand about how she has been feeling. There are also some important messages in Susan's account about the sort of support that is needed and wanted to help people get through the difficulties, problems and emotional crises that they may experience.

Some messages for other people from Susan's story

- Having someone to talk to is very important when you are going through a difficult time.

- It is easiest talking to close family and friends because they know you, understand you and you can trust them.

- Emotional support is as important as practical support. Both kinds are needed.

- Family, friends and other people (e.g. social workers) can help by keeping in close and regular contact when people are experiencing problems. Susan appreciated people taking the initiative to get in touch with her, instead of her having to get in touch with them.

- Being on your own is lonely and frightening when you are not used to it. Offering people company when they want it is important, and helping people to re-establish a social life, by offering to go out with them. Women find it difficult going out on their own, especially at night, when they don't feel safe.

- Breaking up a long term relationship is emotionally painful. Sensitivity is needed by everyone, but perhaps especially by people such as social workers.

- When you break up with a partner 'you need your friends and family round you more than ever'. Friends and family need to rally round, giving support.

All the names in this chapter, except for Susan's, have been changed.

Easy-to-read version

Chapter 17

My story

by Christiane de Burg with Michelle McCarthy and
Geert van Hove

My name is Christiane de Burg. I am a Belgian woman living
in Ghent. I am now 60 years old.

I got married when I was still very young.

My first husband was very violent and beat me a lot. I was pregnant and lost all the babies because he hit me so much.

Then I got married again. We had two daughters.

This was also not a good marriage and this husband hit me as well. When my eldest daughter was a teenager, my husband raped her. This was terrible. I couldn't cope. My children were put into care.

I was very depressed and was put in a psychiatric hospital. It was terrible.

Later, I moved to group home. I shared with four other people. They were nice people, but I did not really like to live in a group.

Now, I live in my own flat. I like it a lot! I am independent. I have support workers.

I have four grandchildren. I see two of them a lot.

I love to spend time with my grandchildren, it makes me very happy.

Messages:

To staff I would say help women step by step and they will learn to do things by themselves.

To other women with learning disabilities, I would say get help straightaway – don't let your problems get too big!

Chapter 17

My story

By Christiane de Burg, with Michelle McCarthy and Geert van Hove

Introduction

Michelle writes: In February 1998, I was working in Belgium and met Geert. I told Geert about this book and he mentioned that he knew a woman with learning disabilities who was a grandmother and who might like to contribute her story to the book. Christiane was asked what she thought and she was keen to get involved. I sent Christiane some questions of the kind of things I thought it would be interesting to talk about for the book and a month or so later I returned to Belgium to meet her. We spent several hours together and, with Geert acting as translator, Christiane told me about her life and gave her opinions on different issues. Although she had been asked to contribute to the book because she was an older woman and because her role as grandmother was important to her, in fact she had many other things to discuss and had much in common with some of the other women in this book.

My discussion with Christiane was taped and after returning to England I transcribed the tapes and pulled together a coherent story. Christiane was then sent a copy and, again with Geert's help as translator, she was able to comment and amend it in any way she wanted to. This, then, is her account, although obviously not her own words, as she does not speak English.

Christiane's thoughts about the book

I think it is a good idea to produce such a book; it can help staff understand women's lives. Supporters often don't listen to people's life stories and people's feelings. Sometimes when I talk to my support workers, it goes in one ear and out the other, or this is what I feel when talking to them. I think it's good to have different topics in this book, especially sexual abuse, as there is a lot of sexual abuse, I know that.

I am very willing to talk about my life, as I want supporters to learn more about people with disabilities. I don't feel ashamed about my life. I can talk about it all without any problems.

Michelle's note: I told Christiane that most of my work with women with learning disabilities was concerned with sexuality and sexual abuse. She then said that because she had experienced sexual abuse herself, this formed some sort of bridge between us and helped her to talk to me.

How I have lived

My name is Christiane de Burg. I am 60 years old. I live in a housing association flat in Ghent. I live alone with some support from a Supported Living Service. They help with paperwork like letters, bills, with getting to doctor's appointments, shopping, solving my problems. They come once or twice a week, but if I am not well, they come more often. I also get a home-help twice a week to help with cooking, cleaning etc. This is a service for anyone who is old or disabled, not anything to do with people with learning disabilities. I think that I can't live on my own without the Supported Living Service, I really need them to help me live on my own.

I have lived on my own since 12th April 1988. Before that I lived in a group home with four other people for about 18 months. I much prefer to live on my own than in the group home. I have more freedom on my own. I can do what I want, go where I want, like social clubs.

When I lived with other people, I had to take them into account and do things with them. I am very happy to live on my own now. But life was not always like this. I have had many different lives!

Before the group home, I was in a psychiatric hospital for one and a half years. I was having problems with my ex-husband and I was forced to go there. It was a terrible period and it's hard to talk about. I still don't agree with the fact that I had to live there. I was forced. Geert [translator] is the one who took me away from the psychiatric hospital, I want to mention that. Geert then came to visit me and invited me to stay for a few days in a small group home, to see if I liked it. I didn't have to think about it for very long and decided I wanted to move in.

For me it has been good to get help from male staff at the Supported Living Service. They have been a good example of kindness and support and how I thought marriage and family life would be, but wasn't. They could have been women workers, but in fact I have had mostly male workers. What matters to me is not whether they are a man or woman, but whether I can trust them. They need to understand that because of my life I need time to trust people.

My second marriage
Before the psychiatric hospital, I lived with my husband. We had two daughters. But something terrible happened. My husband raped our eldest daughter. I found out when the school asked me to come and talk about it. It was a very difficult time. The court decided that my husband had to lose his legal responsibility as father. I was left with all the responsibility as the mother, but because of my learning disability, I was not able to take care of my daughters, so they were taken away. The older daughter was 16 and she went into a group home. The younger one was 14 and she went to a special school, a boarding school. This was a school for children with mild learning disabilities and emotional and behavioural problems. My oldest daughter had a lot of emotional and sexual problems because of what had happened and she stayed in institutional care until she was 21. The youngest did well at school and met a nice boyfriend who she went to live with when she was 18.

Before this thing happened with my husband, I got no help at all with my children. I found looking after them very hard, very stressful and I was depressed a lot. We had terrible lives then. But I coped nearly all the time, except for three months when I was in a psychiatric hospital. The rest of the time I was at home, even though I was depressed. The only support I got was for both the children to go to boarding schools during the week and only come home at weekends. I tried to do my best with the children. Support services did not exist or we weren't aware of them. There was no one, no professionals, no family to help. Even the priests didn't understand. I used to dream of support, but I didn't get it. The only neighbours or friends we had were through my husband. I was really like a servant then, the only contact I had with them was making them coffee, bringing biscuits. So I never had the opportunity for my own friends.

My husband would not have accepted any support from professionals anyway. He was in charge and I was in the second row to him. I had to do what he said and he didn't agree to get support. He wanted to do things on his own. He was a very difficult person to live with because he was an alcoholic and he hit me. It was not a nice marriage. I don't know if he had learning disabilities or not. He was not good with paperwork. He worked in the heating maintenance department of a hospital.

It was a big shock when the children were taken away, because nobody had worried about them before. That decision was as big a shock as finding out what my husband had done to my daughter. I got no support from anyone about my feelings or what I should do. I was still living with my husband and the children had gone. I felt very alone. I was very depressed and had psychiatric problems. So my husband and my GP had me put into a local psychiatric clinic. I didn't agree to it, but I was made to go by law. I felt very bad, because I had a nice house, with a garden. I couldn't stay long at the clinic, because it was very near to our house and my husband kept coming to see me there and this upset me, so we argued and there were always problems.

My husband was taken to court because he raped our daughter, but he was not sent to prison. They removed his civil rights for a temporary period instead [Note: this means that a person can't vote, buy a house, etc.]. At this time, because of my learning disabilities and because I had been brought up in institutions, I was not able to challenge any of this. I did not have the legal competence or the power to do anything about it. And there was nobody to support me. If I had known what to do, I would have done something. But I was on my own and I didn't have the power to do anything against the court or to tell my story. The decisions were taken without my ... without me.

The police advised me to get a divorce, because my husband was so violent and dangerous. But I couldn't get a divorce, because I was in a psychiatric hospital and I didn't have the right to do it then. So I got divorced as soon as I got out into the group home.

My first marriage

This husband I was talking about was my second husband. I feel uncomfortable to talk about the first marriage, because it went wrong. I was only married for 10 months, although I had lived with him for three months before. I got married for the first time when I was quite young and I was working as live-in servant for a doctor's family. I was very naive and I didn't listen to advice. At my special school I hadn't been prepared for life or relationships with men. It was very strict there. So, I was a stupid young girl and I got married. He had been in prison before and he had had his civil rights removed many times because he was in trouble with the law, but I didn't know any of that at the time. He abused me a lot, every day. In the one year we were together, I got pregnant four times and I lost all the babies because he beat me so much. I was taken into hospital all those times when I miscarried the babies, so the social workers there knew my situation very well. After the divorce from my first husband, they helped me. They found me another job as a servant. After I was married I never had the opportunity to go out to work again, because of my health problems. So I was forced to stay at home.

Other women's lives

I did hear of other women who had been abused when I was in the hospitals, but at that time I didn't really think about them or relate to them. My development then was not what it is now. I heard these stories, but I didn't think about those women having the same life as I had. Then, I just had experiences, not ideas. I have said that because of my school I had no preparation for life, I was young and naive. The first time I had sex I had no idea what it was, as I had had no education or preparation.

Now, later in my life, I have thought a lot about why I got abused and why so many women with learning disabilities get abused. I think that some men are really looking for such women. The men are often older than the women, they feel that they can abuse you because they know that your development is not advanced and that you are naive. They take advantage of your naivety, both your emotions and your lack of ability to think about things. They know that thinking about your life, balancing positive and negative things, is not a priority, you just want to be like all the other women, with a boyfriend or husband. You are not aware about dangers. This I think is important, that there are men who are looking for those women especially.

Michelle's note: I tell Christiane that I have come to similar conclusions myself as a result of my work with many women with learning disabilities. Therefore I ask Christiane what can be done about this. What can staff members do to support women with learning disabilities?

Firstly, if the woman has already been abused, the staff must listen to the woman. They must understand the woman's life story and take all her experiences into account, when they give their help. Then they should try to help these women in a very broad sense, practically and emotionally. But this can only be done after they have heard the woman's own story.

But if abuse hasn't happened yet, then this is very hard for staff as young people don't like to listen to advice. They want to do what they want to do! But how staff could help is by trying to form a good relationship with the women or the girls and get their trust. Then tell them about life, about the positive and negative things that could happen to them. Staff should not say 'do that or don't do that' but tell women what the consequences of their decisions will be. But it is very hard to prepare young girls for the evil world. When I was young I didn't listen to any-one, I just said 'it's my life'. But now I look back on it, it would have been good to listen.

Michelle's note: I ask Christiane what she thinks about women with learning disabilities coming together to support each other.

I think groups like this could work, but there would be lots of difficulties. They would need staff to support them, give them guidance. It wouldn't work on its own, there would be fighting and quarrelling. Support is very necessary. But it is important for staff not to impose their power and influence. You can hear in staff's voices when they do this, they shout at you. I don't believe in this. I have had supporters and educators who have done this with me and they didn't influence me at all. If staff want to guide and influence people with learning disabilities they have to build up relationships with people with learning disabilities. They must use a soft voice and listen to people, like real human beings.

Michelle's note: I tell Christiane that men who abuse women with learning disabilities are very rarely prosecuted or punished. I ask her why she thinks this is.

Men hitting women is not a priority in our society. The prisons are already full. I am not an expert, but I think that before they are sent to prison, they should be sent to a centre for education about how to have good relationships with women. Then if they don't change after that, they should go to prison.

Being a mother

When my oldest daughter was born, I was not married yet to the man, but by the time my youngest daughter was born, we had got married. My oldest daughter had emotional and behavioural problems and the youngest one had learning disabilities. They were sent to residential schools, so I felt that as a mother I couldn't do very much for my children, because they were away so much. I was a weekend mother only. My children were not easy to handle because of their own problems. It was very difficult to influence or control them, I felt I didn't have any power as a mother. It is hard for me to think about what I might have done right with them, because they were so hard to handle. I think I was a good mother when I hugged them, when we played games, went for walks. But it's not easy to think about being the mother of two children with problems, also having your own problems. Now when I look back I know that I lost my children, so it's not easy to think about the positive side.

My husband did not help with the children at all, this was all my responsibility. I did everything for them. When the children were home, he would come home from work, sit down and watch television.

I know that there are other mothers with learning disabilities and that they have to cope alone too. But it would be good if they could get support with specific problems. Lots of women with learning disabilities want to have children, just like other women do. Some staff are positive about this, but most are negative. They always think you will have problems. I think that if staff agree with the principle of women with learning disabilities having children, then it's logical that they will need support. It is important to give advice. But it is possible that some women have too many problems to have children.

Michelle's note: Because I am currently working with mothers with learning disabilities who have been to a family centre, I ask Christiane what she thinks about supporting women with learning disabilities in this way.

I think it is better to see people individually and at home, because it is more private. When I have problems I get my help at home and this creates another atmosphere. At centres it is not private and I would be worried that they don't have a real choice. But I know that sometimes children are in danger and so sometimes mothers have to be forced into things. A lot of fathers don't take their responsibility. This was my experience, looking back. Then all the problems are with the mothers. I believe in a system where children would be taken into foster care temporarily, to give the women time to sort out problems with their husbands. That would give the women time to recover and know that they had not lost their children for ever.

Being a grandmother

I have four grandchildren. My oldest daughter has two children, aged two-and-a-half and three-and-a-half. They live a long way away, so I only see them twice a year. My younger daughter also has two children, aged six and eight. They live close by, so I see them at least once a month. I love to see them, it's always very, very nice to see them. I feel like a different person, like I'm reborn, when I'm with my grandchildren. When my grandchildren are with me, it's like little puppies around a mother dog. They are always close by, asking for attention, giving hugs. So I like it very much to have contact with them.

When I was well, the children would come to stay overnight. Now I am not well they just come to visit. I think this is a pity, but it's due to my bad health. The doctors say I shouldn't have them to stay any more, as I don't have the energy. It upsets me that I can't have them to stay any more, because I liked that a lot. It's very different to be a grandmother than a mother and it's easier. I was stricter with my own children. I am more relaxed with my grandchildren. I would have one child at a time to stay and this is better as I can't cope with two.

In the future I know that I won't be able to do so much with my grandchildren, because of my health. What I do now is the best I can do. But little things like hugs are enough, we don't need big plans. I like very much to give presents on their birthdays, Christmas time, etc. But because I don't have much money, it's difficult to give presents. I would like to spoil them. My support staff sometimes criticise when I spend money on the grandchildren, because they say I can't afford it. It upsets me that I can't help my children and grandchildren in the way that I want to, but my physical condition means I can't. So thinking about the future is hard and it upsets me.

My advice to others
To end, I would say that if women with learning disabilities want to become more independent, then:

My message for staff is that the model of the Supported Living Service is best. At first staff will need to take most of the responsibility, but gradually they can give the women more and more responsibility, so they can become more independent.

My message for women themselves is to accept the fact that you need support, before you get too deep into problems. Once you get into problems, you don't make any progress. So accept that you need support.

References

Atkinson, D. and Williams, F. (1990) *'Know Me As I Am'. An anthology of prose, poetry and art by people with learning difficulties.* London, Hodder and Stoughton.

Bayley, M. (1997) *What price friendship? Encouraging the relationships of people with learning difficulties.* Minehead, Hexagon publishing.

Between Ourselves (1988) Video produced and distributed by Twentieth Century Vixen, Brighton.

Bewley, C. (1998) 'Still fighting institutional living', VIA News No. 94

Brown, H. and Turk, V. (1992) 'Defining sexual abuse as it affects adults with learning disabilities', *Mental Handicap*, 20, June: 44–55.

Brown, H., Stein, J. and Turk, V. (1995), 'The sexual abuse of adults with learning disabilities: report of a second two-year incidence survey', *Mental Handicap Research* 8, 1: 3–24.

Brownmiller, S. (1975) *Against our will: men, women and rape.* London, Penguin.

Churchill, J. et al. (eds.) *There Are No Easy Answers.* Chesterfield/Nottingham, ARC/NAPSAC.

Cooper, M. (1997) 'Mabel Cooper's Life Story', in Atkinson, D., Jackson, M. and Walmsley, J. (eds) *Forgotten Lives. Exploring the History of Learning Disability.* Kidderminster, BILD Publications.

Davis, A. et al. (1995) 'To have and have not: addressing issues of poverty', in Philpot, T. and Ward, L. (eds) *Values and Visions: changing ideas in services for people with learning disabilities.* Oxford, Butterworth-Heinemann.

Firth, H. and Rapley, M. (1990) *From acquaintance to friendship. Issues for people with learning disabilities.* Kidderminster, BIMH Publications.

Hard, S. and Plumb, W. (1986) 'Sexual abuse of persons with developmental disabilities. A case study'. Unpublished manuscript.

Johnson, K. and Traustadottir, R. (eds) (forthcoming) *Women with Intellectual Disabilities: Finding a place in the world.*

Kelly, L. (1988) *Surviving Sexual Violence.* Cambridge, Polity Press.

King's Fund Centre (1988) *Ties and connections. An ordinary community life for people with learning difficulties.* London, King's Fund Centre.

London Rape Crisis Centre (1988) *Sexual Violence: the reality for women.* London, Women's Press.

McCarthy, M. (1993) 'Sexual experiences of women with learning difficulties in long-stay hospitals', *Sexuality and Disability* 11, 4: 277–286.

McCarthy, M. (1997) *The sexual experiences and sexual abuse of women with learning disabilities in institutional and community settings.* Unpublished PhD thesis, Middlesex University.

McCarthy, M. (1998) 'Sexual violence against women with learning disabilities', *Feminism and Psychology* 8, 4: 544–551.

McCarthy, M. and Thompson, D. (1997) 'A Prevalence Study of Sexual Abuse of Adults With Intellectual Disabilities Referred For Sex Education', *Journal of Applied Research in Intellectual Disability* 10, 2.

Morris, J. (1991) *Pride against Prejudice.* London, The Women's Press.

Murphy, G. (1997) 'Treatment and Risk Management', in Churchill, J. et al. (eds) *There Are No Easy Answers.* Chesterfield/Nottingham, ARC/NAPS AC.

Namdarkhan, L. (1995) *Women with Learning Disabilities: Mixed Sex Living – Who Benefits?* Unpublished MA Dissertation, Middlesex University.

Open To Abuse. Frontline Scotland programme shown on BBC2, April 1997.

Powerhouse (1996a) 'Power in the house: women with learning difficulties organising against abuse', in Morris, J. (ed) *Encounters with Strangers: feminism and disability*. London, Women's Press.

Powerhouse (1996b) 'What women from Powerhouse say about sexual abuse', *Tizard Learning Disability Review* 1, 4: 39–43.

Randall, M. and Haskell, L. (1995) 'Sexual violence in women's lives: findings from the Women's Safety Project, a community based study', *Violence Against Women* 1, 1: 6–31.

Rapley, M., Kiernan, P. and Antaki, C. (1998) 'Invisible to Themselves or Negotiating Identity? The International Management of "Being Intellectually Disabled"', *Disability and Society* Vol. 13, No. 5: 807–827

Segal, L. (1990) *Slow Motion: changing masculinities, changing men*. London, Virago.

Spelman, E. (1990) *Inessential Woman*. London, The Woman's Press

Thompson, D. and Brown, H. (1997) 'Issues from the Literature', in Churchill, J. et al. (eds) *There Are No Easy Answers*. Chesterfield/ Nottingham, ARC/NAPS AC.

Thompson, D. and Brown, H. (1998) *Response-ability: working with men with learning disabilities who have difficult or abusive sexual behaviours*. Brighton, Pavilion Publishing.

Thompson, P. (1988) *The voice of the past*. Oxford, Oxford University Press.

Walmsley, J. (1993) 'Women First', *Critical Social Policy* Issue 38: 86–100

Walsall Women's Group (1994) *No Means No*. Walsall, Learning For Living Scheme.

Ward, J. (1995) *No Man Has The Right*. Glasgow, Renfrew Zero Tolerance Implementation Team.

Williams, C. (1995) *Invisible Victims: crime and abuse against people with learning disabilities*. London, Jessica Kingsley Publishers.

Williams, F. (1989) 'Mental Handicap and Oppression', in *Making Connections,* ed. Brechin and Walmsley, Hodder and Stoughton.

Zarb, G. (1992) 'On the road to Damascus: first steps towards changing the relations of disability research and practice'. *Disability, Handicap and Society* Vol. 7 No. 2: 125–138.

about **bild**

The British Institute of Learning Disabilities is based in Kidderminster, Worcestershire. Supported by a national membership network of over 1,200 professionals, carers, parents and enablers, BILD is committed to improving the quality of life of people with learning disabilities by advancing education, research and practice and by promoting better ways of working with and for children and adults with learning disabilities. Since its inception in 1972, BILD has become a major provider of training and publisher of books and journals on a wide range of topics relating to learning disabilities.

For more information and a catalogue of BILD publications, contact:

The British Institute of Learning Disabilities
Wolverhampton Road
Kidderminster
Worcestershire DY10 3PP
Telephone: 01562 850251
Fax: 01562 851970
e-mail: bild@bild.demon.co.uk

BILD is a Company limited by guarantee, No. 2804429
Registered as a charity No. 1019663